Gwen Ran

Help! I

a parent!

HOW TO COPE IN THE FIRST YEAR

Gwen Rankin

Help! I'm a parent!

HOW TO COPE IN THE FIRST YEAR

First published in 1988 by
Judy Piatkus (Publishers) Ltd,
5 Windmill Street, London W1P 1HF

Revised paperback edition 1994

Originally published as *The First Year*

*A catalogue record for this book is
available from the British Library*

ISBN 0 7499 1382 7

Illustrations by Helen Chown B.A. (Hons) Fine Art
Front cover illustration by John Henson

Phototypeset in Linotron Times by
PDB Ltd, London SW17
Printed and bound in Great Britain by
Biddles Ltd, Guildford & King's Lynn

For my grandchildren

Contents

THE BABY'S FIRST YEAR

NEW PERSPECTIVES ON PARENTING

Introduction

This book is written from experience, not theory. I would not have dared to write it thirty years ago, when I was in the midst of learning about early parenthood for myself, having our five children. Like most young parents I was bombarded with theories — and had to find my own way of exploding them or agreeing with them. It was during that time that I learned to think about parenting from the baby's point of view, as well as my own.

Nor would I have dared to write a book simply from my own experience. That is individual, and conditioned by my particular partner in parenthood — my husband — and his upbringing, my upbringing, our lifestyle, and the country and times in which we live. But I have been fortunate in being an antenatal teacher, and so have heard and shared the experiences of so many hundreds of other parents, from all walks of life.

Hearing the thoughts and concerns of parents-in-the-making during pregnancy and in the first few months after the birth of their babies has widened my understanding. I have observed many varied approaches to childbirth and babycare, and being always in touch with young mothers and fathers has kept me from thinking that my ways were the only ways! It has made me keep abreast of changes and jolted me to think afresh, time and time again.

Out of all this have emerged some constant concerns, which

seem to be relevant to all new parents and their babies, however society's attitude may change. It would be easy to fill a book with the difficult, negative aspects of new parenthood such as tiredness, anxiety, stress — financial and emotional — crying and depression, and these must never be ignored. But from all these young parents the positive side shines through: delight and warmth of emotion, sudden surprise at the richness of family life, growth of confidence and love. Perhaps the joys do not get enough of the headlines at this time.

The sense of panic which you may feel when you are about to become a parent is only natural. Bringing a new person into the world — a person with whom you will share your life — means that things will change! In this book I want to help you to prepare for the reality of having a baby. I hope you will read *Help! I'm a parent!* before you have your baby and that you will find it both helpful and reassuring. Having a first baby is a whole new experience. One of joy, with a little panic and fear thrown in!

For all new parents, one way to cope with the bewilderment of the first few weeks after birth is through compassion for the baby, who has the most bewildering time of all. It is for the three of you — the mother, the father and the baby — that this book is written.

Before the birth

It is in pregnancy that you have time to read books, and think about the arrival of your baby, and wonder what your life is going to be like as a family. At the beginning of pregnancy your own physical feelings seem to exclude everything else. Then you start to think about the baby, and often have anxious feelings about how you will react to being a mother, how your partner will like being a father, and whether you will miss being at work. Some pregnant women say they fear feeling 'trapped' when their baby arrives, and are scared of leaving their familiar work behind. One wise antenatal teacher I know answers this fear by saying, 'OK, you feel a door may be closing behind you when your baby arrives. But the room you're going into has another door which is open a crack, and you only have to push it and there's a new, bigger, brighter room which is for you and the baby together.'

Whatever anxieties you may have in pregnancy, which will be unique to you, it is helpful to read widely, and also to look for really good antenatal classes. There, you will meet other couples who are at the same stage of pregnancy as yourself. They may come from different walks of life, but they will be facing just the same questions and worries. Sharing these in a group where you can talk freely, and find out all that you can about childbirth and the baby's first few weeks, is always a help. You don't feel alone any more.

Preparation for parenthood is never out of date. People go on having babies, and every woman expecting her first baby has a new set of questions to ask. Every man about to become a father for the first time has equally profound feelings, and used not to be expected to admit his fears and worries, or even his curiosity about birth. Those days are thankfully past and there is now plenty of information available for men and women before the birth of their baby.

Considering the options

Birth at home as a real choice had nearly disappeared in Britain by the 1970s. But some midwives and many parents believed very strongly that having a baby in your own comfortable surroundings, attended by a midwife whom you know well throughout your pregnancy, and without the stress of having to move during labour to unfamiliar places and people, was worth campaigning for. As a result, the option of home birth is coming back into favour for women who have 'low risk' pregnancies.

Hospital is the right place for women with special problems, such as high blood pressure or a history of previous difficulties — and there is still a preference for first babies to be born in hospital. But in some places there are now teams of independent domiciliary midwives who are experienced in home deliveries and book their own patients, under the cover of a local hospital in case of emergencies. General practitioners may also book patients for home birth, especially if they have a midwife attached to the practice who has experience of attending births at home.

Childbirth fashions change, and nowhere more so than in the relief of labour pain. Before Queen Victoria used chloroform for the birth of one of her many babies, there were herbal medicines such as opium to ease pain, and others to accelerate the birth. But the use of chloroform by so revered and public a figure heralded a spate of interventions which have proved more or less effective for relief of labour pain — 'twilight sleep', 'gas and air', trilene, pethidine ('demarol' in North America), pethilorfan, heroin, and diamorphine, to name but a few. Each comes into favour and may be used widely, only to have its use modified because of the effects on the baby being born.

A different approach came when a British doctor, Grantly Dick-Read, looked carefully at women in normal labour, and concluded that *much* of their pain was due to tension caused by fear of the unknown. So he started to teach his patients about the course of labour, and how and why to relax and breathe helpfully during birth. By co-operating with their working bodies, rather than resisting what they felt, they might reduce pain. His Ignorance — Fear — Tension — Pain syndrome made sense to women who eagerly grasped the chance to understand their labours and give birth free from fear.

The benefits of *knowledge* were clear, and women started to share their skills and experience with pregnant friends and neighbours. This was the start of the preparation for childbirth classes which are now available for all who want them. Classes are now offered by all maternity hospitals, by many clinics, and many charitable trusts of which the National Childbirth Trust was the pioneer. (See page 191.)

New methods of pain relief followed, aimed at keeping the mother awake and aware, rather than doped and confused. The approaches divided, some to more extreme use of drugs by epidural or spinal injections, which have also proved to affect the baby; others towards more active response to labour, use of movement and gravity, 'tens' (transcutaneous nerve stimulus), and the soothing effect of a warm bath.

Water births are now much in demand, and like all other interventions in labour, need to be wisely used. Lying in water a little above body temperature eases pain, but the benefit of upright movement is lost. Anyone who has had a baby in a hot and humid part of the world knows how much easier it is to relax there, but also knows the danger of *over*heating. So the temperature of the bath should be varied and the time spent in the bath carefully watched. Once again, information and understanding are the key to helpful results.

When talking about water births a distinction must be made between *labouring* in warm water, and *delivery* in warm water. If, during the labour, the mother has passed urine or faeces into the water there are obvious risks to the baby's eyes and mouth if she or he is born under the water, and might possibly try to take the first breath before being lifted clear into air. Many babies have successfully been born under water if the second stage of labour has been very rapid, but the most frequent practice now is for the mother to use the water bath for part of the first stage of labour and get out of it for the delivery of the baby.

Anxiety and Reality

At the start of the longstanding debate on childbirth the emphasis was entirely on the birth. Women were fed up with being treated like objects when they laboured. They demanded the right to have a say in their treatment, and to choose where to give birth to their babies, and with what kind of pain relief, if any. They wanted to learn the art of breastfeeding without tears. They wanted information on the difficulties of the first few days after the birth.

You can see how preparation for parenthood has grown in content and complexity in response to the questions and wishes of the expectant parents. The style of antenatal classes has changed in the same way. When learning about labour was something you were hardly expected to ask for or talk about, the teacher *taught* and then answered questions. Very soon the questions and voicing of anxieties proved far more important than any formal teaching, so the groups became more and more informal, while still covering all the essential skills for giving birth.

Now antenatal teachers are trained to listen and learn, as well as to share all the knowledge they possess. They are there to discuss childbirth with parents, who bring their own awareness and experience, rather than to *tell* the group what they should do. Teachers, such as myself, who have taught continuously over the last thirty years, would hardly recognize the classes they once gave; modern groups are so much more valuable. Yet I believe that the aftermath to giving birth is still comparatively untaught, the anxieties often unexpressed in advance. And hence the need for a book such as this.

It is no wonder that after a baby is safely born, and mother and baby are back home and on their own, the parents suffer a definite feeling of deflation. They are no longer of such importance to their doctors and midwives. The crisis time for the medical people is past. But for the mother and father the really long-term hard work is only just beginning; the demands on them have increased beyond their imagination. Their anxiety is just as strong as it was before, but they cannot help but feel abandoned — left to deal with it as best they may. In Britain the midwife's daily (statutory) visit stops when the baby is ten days old, and the health visitor only has to make one visit to check that all is well. Of course they are there to be contacted if there is a problem, but many people *don't* because they don't want to be thought to be worrying unnecessarily. It can be a lonely time.

Parents very soon realise that the neat idea that school age is going to be the end of their total involvement with their child is a myth. A child — children — are your family, for *all* your life — not just a few short years. You think of yourself growing up in a family and you know that the family is part of you, for ever. You see clearly that the family your baby is going to grow up in is very important indeed. And it dawns on you that creating a new family is now *your* job, and nobody else's.

If this realization hits you when you are surrounded by supporting and loving people you will probably take it in your stride. But if it hits you when things are hard, and you're alone, and the baby is crying and you're tired, then no wonder you may become depressed. It takes time to get back to full energy after such a big physical event as giving birth to a baby, and it takes time to get used to becoming a family — and we are not good at taking time in this quick-moving and demanding age.

Most families are separated from their wider families by the demands of jobs, so the natural support that they would once have sought is often removed from them by circumstances. For some couples this is a blessing: if you *can't* turn to your mother or aunt or father or sister to help you out when the going is rough, you *have* to find your own strengths and rely on your own friends much more quickly.

For other couples, being deprived of wider family support when their first baby is born is the hardest thing of all, especially if one or other of them has little or no experience of happy childhood and few, if any, role models to draw from in giving security to their child.

But underlying all the adjustments you will have to make is a great happiness. After your baby is born, you have the deeply satisfying joy of having grown, and given birth to an amazing little creature. This feeling of achievement — and, for many parents, sense of wonder — will remain with you as you and your baby learn about each other.

Often it may be difficult to remember to be 'happy'. In the crowded hours of each day, there is so much to do for the helpless newcomer. But in the quiet moments you feel that your life has changed beyond belief, and that the baby is a miracle. In this book it is important to look clearly at the difficult aspects of life with a new baby, so you are, in a small way, prepared. But all through the first year, the happiness and joy of being a parent goes hand in hand with the demands.

After the rush of the first few weeks, the delight in the baby increases. His growth, her smiles, the response every time you appear, teaches you how important you are to your baby. The laughs are pure delight, and your sense of achievement grows day by day. Having another person to love is the reason — and *such* a person, one who is glad to see you without qualification or complication! Love dwindles if you keep it to yourself, and one of the amazing paradoxes is that the more love you pour out, the more you have to give. An extra person, very small, very valuable, and very close to you, is easy to love and will enrich your life.

The sudden bubbling up of this new loving can be quite a

surprise. It can come immediately the baby is born, at the moment of birth, or more slowly over the days or weeks following the birth. It varies from woman to woman, and birth to birth. Parenthood may be hard work and full of responsibilities, but it is worth every minute. It is probably the most important and influential job any of us ever do. Our children are the future.

The great divide

The arrival of your first child is a watershed in your life. As you grow up from babyhood to childhood to adulthood you go through many rites of passage from one state to the next. Your first day at your first school moves you from pre-school to school age; your first love changes you from someone mainly concerned with yourself to someone for whom another person is equally important; your wedding turns you from an unmarried to a married woman or man, accepting and promising responsibilities; your first pregnancy moves you from little contact with children to inevitable involvement with them; your first birth makes you a parent — for ever. It doesn't stop there — middle age, bereavement, old age, retirement, death, all have their rites of passage. If you ignore these watersheds you can get into all sorts of muddles — physically, mentally, and spiritually.

Birth is the watershed that women cannot ignore. It is a bodily process that you simply cannot stop, once it starts. You can delay sleeping or eating or talking, but once birth is under way it will go on until the baby is born. It is that instinctive knowledge of inevitability that scares so many women in their first pregnancy and makes them feel they need to seek some — any — way out. Good information and preparation helps a very great deal, but every woman goes into birth alone and experiences her own unique rite of passage, which may be exactly as she expected, or worse, or better.

I talked with a young, new mother who is at this watershed.

> **Kate** 'When you are first pregnant you never really know what's ahead. I didn't want to think about the birth until I was at least six months pregnant. I didn't read any books until then, and not much after that. My big fear was not giving birth to a healthy baby, and I kept hearing about miscarriages and stillbirths. I'd fixed the date they gave me firmly in my mind, and when I went over that by a week, and then two weeks, the worries got worse. There was a TV programme about babies with big problems during that time and I really didn't believe I'd have a baby without difficulties, however much James kept saying, 'Think of all the thousands of babies who are normal.' So when Archie was born, and he was all right, it was just fantastic! A simply marvellous feeling, which hasn't worn off yet after three weeks.'

What fathers can do

Expectant fathers also look for help about birth. It is now acceptable for fathers to be present when their babies are born, though this might not be the initial choice of some men! I have heard of one hospital where having fathers present at the births was such a success that they have made it *compulsory* for every father to attend his partner in labour! That is as wrong as having a rule that *no* fathers may be present at their child's birth. The mother giving birth must have the final say, since *she* is experiencing the labour — for some that will be made easier by having the father there, while for others it will not.

If a father *is* going to be there with her through the birth, he needs to be a participant, not merely an onlooker. There is nothing more uncomfortable than feeling in the way in a busy group. Preparation for childbirth classes varies a great deal in value, but almost all now pay at least lip service to the needs of fathers by including one 'father's evening' in the course. This will offer information about labour, pain relief, the appearance of the newborn, and possibly a film of a birth. For many men this is not nearly enough. The film may be off-putting; the visual impact of watching a baby emerging from the midwife's end of the bed on film is not what he will see if he is there at the time. His place will be at the mother's head, encouraging and helping her.

The best pre-birth classes include the fathers in most, if not all, of the classes — *if* they want to come. They can then join in all discussion, ask their own questions, understand their partner's anxieties and needs, and learn the relaxation and breathing skills which are so helpful for life as well as labour. In many classes I taught it was the men who asked most questions, once the design and function of birth interested them. Their fear of 'pain and blood' changed to varying degrees of enthusiasm for helping their women give birth free from fear. I found that one evening for fathers was never enough, and if possible the men wanted to attend the whole course. In the end I had to make sure there was at least one evening for mothers alone!

My son-in-law, John, went to couples classes before the birth of his first baby — and when his second was on the way he wanted a 'refresher class'. A civil engineer, he was then working on a project far from his home, so he looked for the nearest National Childbirth Trust class to where he worked. He asked if he could join as a lone father, for at least some of the classes on breathing for labour. The teacher agreed, with some trepidation because she gave classes for mothers only. John was quite unworried by being the only man there, and the other class members soon accepted him as an experienced father. An unexpected result was that the teacher went on to include the fathers in all her classes — if they wanted to be there.

Men understand quickly what an athletic experience birth is! The co-ordination of muscle action, and the need for a steady oxygen supply to those muscles makes sense of the regular practice of breathing and relaxation which helps so much when the time comes. Classes are like rehearsals, and fathers can help a great deal.

I asked some fathers, who had been to classes before their babies' births, how they remembered being there.

Andrew 'It was exciting, and *very* emotional, especially at the wonderful moment when the baby emerged after all the effort and patience. Part of the time I felt useful and part of the time in the way — about fifty-fifty. But I wouldn't have missed it for anything.'

John 'I've been there at all three births. The first two were in hospital and it was great to be along. It was most important to be eyes and ears for her, and an intermediary between her and the midwives — sometimes she could only hear me, not them. The third was fantastic because it was at home, and I was the first person to hold the baby. That was very special.'

Harry 'It was interesting to see the process, and very important to be a support — it was such a quick labour. No rests, and so tiring. But the wonder of the baby didn't hit me until we brought him home — that was amazing.'

The watershed for women

Women say that the experience of giving birth is total and overwhelming; so they are always extremely glad to have come out the other side, and relieved to have completed the experience. Their initial reaction may be to sleep and sleep, or to take time to catch their breath and get feelings into proportion, or to get up and waltz around the room feeling light and bright. Much depends on their own bodies, the conduct of the birth, and the quality of the support they have received.

But immediately after childbirth women find that they have gained a link with every other woman who has had a baby. You have joined a sisterhood; you are made free of an understanding and a camaraderie which you did not have before.

Nevertheless, it is not only the experience of birth which totally changes your life. It is the baby. It is the experience and expectations of the baby from birth on that change you. This is the great divide, and the big difference between men and women. Men never *have* to subject themselves totally to another person's wishes — women with a baby do. A man may *choose* to do so, but a woman with a baby cannot choose. She is involved with her baby from the moment of birth.

What does this experience of inevitability do for women? Apart from the initial feelings of achievement and panic, which is a heady cocktail, each day you live with your baby, love him, suffer with her, change his nappies, soothe her colic, rock him to sleep, push her out in the pram, feed him, cuddle her, comfort him, protect her, smile at him, laugh with her, you are becoming a parent, growing into a new fully-fledged state of life. Asking women to look back and tell me what becoming a parent had done for them, and how they thought they had changed, I got some significant responses.

> **Nancy** 'I thought life would carry on the same as before when the birth was over; I was quite determined it would. I said to my mother, "I'm not going to change a bit when this baby arrives — it's got to fit in with *my* life, and I won't be soggy about it like so many women are." What a laugh — she changed my life totally, and straight away. That tremendous overwhelming feeling of responsibility — I can understand completely how some women can't cope and find it all too much. I'm much stronger for having a child; it's a matter of fighting for someone else without question — the first time I ever felt like that. The first time I really experienced protectiveness, and it now extends to all other little children as well as my own, and animals too. I don't mind how dirty or noisy or disruptive children are, they are still little people to me, a part of my race and my species. Having a child has made me belong to the human race.

'I was awfully judgemental before — now I've learned not to be. I know why people get overstressed and strained, from my own experience, and what strengths you have to develop. Another thing, it forces you to accept that there aren't always answers to questions — no slick solutions to problems. It's very freeing to be able to say you don't know how to handle something, and learn how to wait for a solution. It's increased my disappointment with men though; they constantly fail to show the ability to be grown-up people, and they duck out of responsibility over and over again. They miss so much of being a parent right out.'

Judy 'I'd always been successful, and because good results were easy to come by, in exams and suchlike, I was always disappointed that that was all that people expected of me — it didn't give me great confidence; that has come through producing children. They're so super that I *know* it's good to have borne them.

'My first pregnancy and birth was maximum misery. That was the first time I couldn't *make* things go well; I'd never felt so hopeless and helpless. It was a very useful time to me, because I learned the need to have support from other people, and the warmth of other human contacts. I'll never forget the sudden overwhelming love I felt for the baby. I knew then that I had the stamina to protect her and I'd kill anyone who hurt her; she gave me my courage and strength back. I knew I had an ally — I remember the moment of looking at her and saying "OK, it's you and me, girl." I feel that way about my husband too now, but it took a lot longer.

'I'm extremely proud of myself because I'm good at being a parent. I know that what I've done is good enough, because the children are great. Through being a parent I've come to realize the importance of joining with other people — you can't do anything as a person in the world on your own. The world is not set up to make things nice and good for people, and you can't make changes on your own without other people. One alone and the system gets you. Two or three gathered together can make an impression.'

Christine 'Having a child has forced me to be much more patient. I've had to slow down a lot. You can't plan for things in the same way you could before the baby was born; you have to grab opportunities when they arise. I savour going out in the evenings now, on the rare occasions when we can.

'My son has made me go back to simplicity — teaching and learning with him. It's fascinating when he cottons on to something; a week after I've said something to him he suddenly brings it out, and I realize he's taking everything in all the time.

'At the start you can fit the baby into your life, but after a while you can't any more, because the baby is a person with his own life, his own will, and you have to recognize that and give the baby room to be himself and have his own boundaries. You want him to grow up to be independent, so you must let him make choices and decisions, at least sometimes. Babies and toddlers learn slowly to accept that they need to fit into their parents' lives too.

'Time by myself is very precious now. Just sitting and doing nothing, or reading. Tiredness and lack of uninterrupted sleep is still my biggest problem. He brings moments of absolute pure joy which are extraordinary. We were both amazed one Sunday, watching him spend the whole day figuring out how to get from sitting in the middle of the floor to standing up. He wouldn't try walking or anything until he had mastered that. It was astonishing.'

Kim 'The biggest change in me is that I've got more patience now. My husband didn't want children and was horrified when I was pregnant. We'd lived in our tidy, orderly house for several years, and now it was all going to be turned upside down. He's terrified of babies, but likes children, so I knew he'd have nothing to do with the baby after he was born. I stopped work a few weeks before the birth, and hated that time. I missed my job, and I was very, very overweight and couldn't move easily, and all my friends warned me that I'd have postnatal depression.

'But I didn't. The first few weeks were awful, with an unhappy stay in hospital and then desperate tiredness when I came home. I breastfed him until 15 weeks, and then put him on the bottle. He slept better after that, and *I* got some sleep and felt fine again. I loved his company — I'm never lonely now. But I felt harassed by my neighbours on the estate. Neighbours are always watching everything you do, and expect you to be the same as everyone else. One day my next-door neighbour said "I see you've got *twenty-four* nappies on the line! Most of us only put out a few at a time!" I said "So?" and didn't see why I should explain that I'd bought a washing machine and I liked to save up lots of nappies to do a big wash after several days rather than a few every day. We've moved now, and it's better on our own. We can do things in our own time. My husband and son get on fine now.'

Jan 'I'm much more mature now. I always said I didn't want children. I loved them when they belonged to other people, but I didn't want the responsibility of my own all the time. But I've coped as a parent *much* better than I thought I would. I come from a big family and always had kids around, so I suppose it was inevitable. There's no right or wrong time for me; I didn't want any just after we were married — I wanted time to get used to that. But after a couple of years I began to think it would be rather nice.

'Now I'd like to have lots of children, and give them the close family I had. But I won't, because of the lack of time. We're so busy with our business every day, and there's not enough time available for the kids even now. I'm not really a career woman, and I'd happily just be a mother. With our first child I spent the whole day with her and read to her a lot and played with her. But with this second one I simply haven't the time to do the same, and I feel guilty about that. He's fine and healthy and happy, but I have to leave a lot of his entertainment to my wider family nearby. Our kids will have to make do with lots of cousins.'

Laura 'Having the baby made me grow up — they do, don't they? The change in your life is so complete, and I'd been used to being very busy and flying about all the time. When the baby arrived I had to stop haring around. It didn't seem very strange to me — there was no depression about it, because I'm the eldest of a big family, with a very busy mother, and used to having younger children around, and caring for them. My parents had five children in eight years, and then a late baby born when I was fourteen, and my sisters and I all think we learnt our baby-care on him. We loved him and loved helping with him. So handling a baby wasn't difficult.

'I had a very demanding job, but I don't miss it — yet. We've moved three times already for jobs, and I hope we stay put for a bit now. Life with small kids is interesting, and so important. You learn patience very quickly, and how not to panic over small disasters.'

Alice 'I never imagined life without children. It would have been a shock to find I couldn't have a baby. Having them has given me much more confidence and opened up a different aspect on life, watching how they grow, and seeing how I can help them. Parents are all that children have as guidelines, to start with, so it's a big responsibility. They've made me very happy and very whole. Being a mother has brought more tiredness than I knew existed! And frustrations and worries too. But you can't have happiness without that — you'd never recognize it.'

THE BIRTH OF YOUR BABY

The idea of change

It takes quite a few weeks to get used to the changes in your life that a new baby brings. This is obviously most marked with a first baby. Just for fun, there are some simple things you can do before the baby is born to give you some idea of what changes to expect. Take a large piece of paper and draw two circles on it, divided up into two 24-hour clocks. With your partner, fill in the wedges in one circle with your daily activities — eight hours sleep, half an hour for breakfast, an hour's travel, so many hours at work, meals, bath, going out, talking to friends, family visiting, entertainment, etc. It's quite difficult to find an average of your activities together, and fun to see how your 24-hour circle divides up.

Then fill in your second circle, imagining that the baby has been born and taking into account the baby's needs. The baby will need feeding every two or three hours in its first week or two, sometimes through the night as well as the day. It must be bathed, and have its clothes changed, and the clothes must be washed for next day. In the first few days back home allow for the midwife, doctor and health visitor to call at some time each day. And so on, until you have filled in all the things you can think of that the baby needs to have done. Then look at your second 24-hour clock and see what the differences are compared with your first one. Usually this is quite an eye-opener for busy young parents expecting their first baby.

It's not only your own days and nights which will immediately be affected by the arrival of the baby. All your family ties and close relationships will change subtly because of your new son or daughter.

Another game you can play before the birth is to take a handful of coins from your purse or pocket, and select two of them to represent you, the two parents, and place them side by side. Then arrange other coins around 'you' with appropriate spacial variety according to the closeness or importance of the people who matter to you both; your own parents, who may be near or far — not so much in geographical terms but in their friendship and interest — sisters or brothers, friends, neighbours, bosses or workmates, even pets if you have a dog or a cat who is very much part of your family.

Now take a small coin to represent the baby. He or she has been born — where does the baby fit in to your arrangement? Close to both of you? Closer to one of you? Between you — which means a bit more space between you? What happens to the other coins when the baby is fitted in? Do they get closer round you, supporting you? Or do some of them get less important and fade out further? What happens to the dog and the cat? Do they get pushed out? Does your mother or your mother-in-law suddenly get much closer to you? What about your father or your father-in-law? Will either of you feel more closely identified with them? Or one of them?

You can anticipate quite a lot of possibilities by playing this very lightheartedly, just thinking ahead to many future shifts in relationships, without being sure about any of them. It can make you less surprised about any of the changes that happen after the baby is born.

Getting to know your baby

However much you have thought ahead and tried to anticipate areas of strain which could affect your enjoyment of the newborn baby, the one thing you cannot anticipate is what sort of personality the baby will be born with. The impact of each baby will vary according to the way he or she settles into life outside the mother's body. When your first baby arrives and proves to be a grand sleeper, quietly adapting to the changes, taking to breastfeeding easily, and reaching the milestones of smiles and laughs and sitting up at the usual times, it is easy to assume that this is all your doing, and that the way you handled the baby was the way all babies should be handled to achieve this desirable result. Not so. The next baby, whom you handle in exactly the same way, may not sleep well at all, may cry a lot and be more difficult to console, be quickly frustrated, wanting to crawl before he can sit up, walk before he can crawl, and talk before everything. It's a different baby, a different child, a new challenge in finding the best way to help him understand and grow.

The opposite can and does happen. You may find your first baby is the one who finds life hard to settle to, gives you endless sleepless nights and seems to want something, anything, different from what you are offering, but is not quite sure what. It is so easy to blame personality on being a *first* baby, and feel guilty about the inexpert way you feel you are handling the baby and the situation. Your next baby may be temperamentally much more adaptable, and you can think it is because you now know what needs to be done, and are more expert at doing it.

If you shift the emphasis away from how you are performing as a standard mother, or father, and towards finding out about the temperament of this new little person you have created together, with interest in the baby's abilities rather than worries about yours, life becomes much happier. With a first baby you are all three quite new to it, so no wonder you all need support and encouragement. The baby, after all, has not read any of the books about baby behaviour; he or she can only be themselves.

You may have read one of many theories, or have very strong views for or against the way you have been brought up in early childhood. Theories are fine — so long as you are prepared to change, modify, or abandon them if they do not suit the baby, or you as a family. The guideline is always to watch the baby. If after the first muddled and confused few days the baby is sleeping well (even though not at set times yet), is feeding well, and is producing healthy motions, then all is well, however unorthodox your handling of the baby is. If any of those things are not going well, then there is need for adaptation, however neat your long-held theories are.

It is so tempting to attribute your baby's behaviour to just one factor, which you feel sure is the reason. For example, if you have had a difficult labour you may see that as the one reason why your baby is restless, or very sleepy. You may be quite correct, but it could be that the baby's own inborn personality is making itself known from the very start, or it may be a combination of all these factors.

Coming home from hospital

It can feel very strange to walk back into your house after the birth. When you walked out of it a few days ago you were in labour, conscious of timing and full of excitement and apprehension, very much in a state of heightened awareness. Now you walk back in with your baby in your arms, and it looks familiar and yet unfamiliar. Some women are still on a wonderful 'high', but many say they experience a sudden — short lived — sinking of the heart and realize that now they have to take up their everyday lives again.

This is partly because the time of great experience, the actual arrival of the baby, has taken place in the hospital, and you always have a visual memory of that background when you think of your first sight of him or her. When you come home, new connections with the visible baby have to be made. Also, even if you have only been in hospital for a very few hours, you have experienced help at your elbow all the time if you have any queries or problems. Back at home you miss that, and understandably may feel alone and insecure. One of the joys of having a baby at home is that you do not have this break in continuity of your familiar surroundings. The baby belongs in your home from the moment it's born.

The first few days after birth are usually very peaceful for the baby, who will be sleeping a great deal of each 24 hours, adjusting to the new situation, getting over the shock of being born, and gradually getting used to the feelings of sucking, swallowing and digesting. It is after the colostrum (see page 92), when the first milk comes in to the mother's breasts, about three days after the birth, that the baby often begins to be alert and wake up to its surroundings, and express its needs more positively. And in our system this is very often the time when the mother and baby leave the hospital and go home!

So the very moment when you really need knowledgeable help around you, and extra hands to help you, and someone to reassure you that all is well, is the moment when you find yourself on your own. In the hospital you have company, other mothers and experts to refer to if the baby cries or looks uneasy, and this can be very helpful.

It is worth thinking before the birth about the family and friends to whom you can turn. You may be in a different county or a different country from your parents or relatives, and in unfamiliar territory for support networks. So find out what organizations are active in your area, as well as making friends of your own who live near you and share your interests. (See Page 191 for a list of organizations who give postnatal help.) The midwife will visit for ten days after the baby's birth, and she and the health visitor are always there if you need them. And baby clinics can be excellent centres for friendship and advice, if there is one in your area.

Husbands and partners are special cases, and you may be a couple who quite definitely prefer to be alone together with your baby for the first days back at home after the birth. Many women like to have other women around when they have given birth. Or you may like to have extra support from your extended family, or a substitute extended family made up of friends whom you know and trust. Friends you can talk to and turn to for sudden help or advice are worth their weight in gold at this time.

One thing you can be certain about is that when you have had a baby you *will* get lots of advice. Whether you want it or not, you will have hints or guidelines or downright rules offered to you. The midwives (who may or may not have had babies of their own), the doctors, the health visitor, your GP, your mother, your mother-in-law, your sisters and brothers, your friends, or any passer-by in the street, will all be ready to tell you what you should be doing and what you are doing wrong. Sometimes even what you are doing right (very encouraging, this) and usually what they did in such a situation! New mothers and fathers sometimes feel absolutely snowed under with advice, and don't know what to do with it all.

The best way to deal with advice is to thank everyone for their kindness in offering you their ideas, whether you asked for them or not, and whether you agree with it or not. Never, never argue! When you are handling a small baby, and have just been through giving birth, you are in a very vulnerable state and disagreement could make you feel hot and sweaty and very able to burst into tears.

Having got the advice, decide whether you think it's good or not. If it is, try it, and see whether it works for you and your baby. If it does, fine — that's a help to you. If it doesn't, discard it — that's no good for your family. If you instinctively don't agree with it, don't even try it, simply put it aside. Later on that bit of advice may be just what you need — or perhaps with another sort of child it might be relevant.

Understanding your feelings

It is important to be able to look back on your labour with understanding. To be able to sort out the good bits and the bad bits, and see why this happened and why that would have been better avoided. The more you understand, the more interested you become in this unique life experience and the less it seems like an endurance test which you will wish to forget as quickly as possible. The same is true of life with baby; the more you know about tiny children and how interesting they can be, and the interests and hazards of the first days after birth, the less frightening those first few weeks ahead of you will be.

It is in these first days after the birth that the course of the labour you have had makes a great deal of difference to your physical feelings. Because of changes in the management of labour by obstetric techniques, many women have stitches in the vagina, and these are the major source of discomfort or outright pain after the baby is born. If you have had them you may need to be prepared for some complications with handling your baby. Pain and dragging discomfort make you much more tired than you would otherwise be, and looking after a new baby is tiring on its own.

VISITORS

Discourage visitors in the first few days. That sounds odd, because of course so many loving relatives and friends will want to come and see the baby and hear about the birth and give presents and congratulations — and you're glad to see them. But however glad you are, after about ten minutes you will find you are tired of talking and want to rest. You are, after all, adjusting to a very big life change, and you can't cope with extras — even of normal conversation.

The best visitors are the ones who come, congratulate you, let you know they love you and are very pleased, and then depart happily. The worst visitors are the ones who call soon after you get home, and settle down for a long chat. They expect *you* to make *them* a cup of tea or supply them with a drink or food, never noticing that you are looking pale and tired, even though the baby may be asleep. Fathers have every right to turn such visitors out!

It might be a good thing to have house rules about visitors in these early days — 'Yes, she'd love to see you, but I'm limiting visits to a quarter of an hour' is an acceptable line. And if visitors object to that, then they do not understand the needs of a new parent, and need not come.

Of course, the visitor who comes not to talk but to help by wading into the housework or taking the baby for a walk in its pram so that the mother can get a sleep is as welcome as the day is long! Friends such as that are invaluable.

A LITTLE MOTHERING

New mothers with their first babies need mothering themselves. They need comfort and support in what they are doing, and reassurance that it *will* get easier and that the baby is doing well. The best person to supply this is their husband or lover, because his encouragement and involvement means more than anyone else's. If he withdraws from her, leaving her emotionally alone, or criticizes her for failing to do everything as efficiently as she did before she had the baby, she will be more vulnerable to depression and problems with the baby than she ever could be under lack of support from any other person. On the other hand, if he has patience for these first few days, encourages her to be with the baby a lot, takes over the daily chores — without martyrdom — if she is tired, and praises her and the baby, it will be surprising how quickly she gains confidence and regains her poise. An ounce of practical help is worth a pound of pity at this time. Little things like the boring ironing, washing up, bed-making and floor cleaning assume enormous proportions when you are extra tired and feeling the weight of new responsibilities.

READJUSTING

After the first few muddled weeks, some order does begin to emerge, and for most new parents that is a wonderful relief. You wake up one morning feeling that life is under your control once more, and that being a parent is good and worthwhile. This often coincides with the baby's first laugh, the most endearing gurgling chuckle, which is set off by some movement or expression or action of yours, and which is as much a surprise to the baby as it is to you. It's a very happy moment, which happens to fathers as well as mothers, often at different times, and makes you realize that the baby is growing and responding under your care.

It is interesting that there are parallels between the nine months after the baby is born and the nine months before. For many women the first three months of pregnancy are not very pleasant; emotionally you are up and down, because your hormones are rebalancing and your body is adjusting to making a baby, and this often makes you feel nauseous on top of the anxieties about relationships and money and jobs. In this time all the fixed things in your life are beginning to change, and you have feelings of insecurity and introspection which you may never have expected to face. Most women also feel that they cannot be sure that the pregnancy is going to continue, until after the first three months are past, because they are aware that many miscarriages happen at about twelve weeks.

The first three months after the baby is born are much the same. The need for both parents is to adapt to a new and urgent situation, and a change in physical lifestyle; the woman's hormones are readjusting, and her feelings about sexuality and lovemaking will be very muddled and unpredictable. In both three months there are new demands on her body, and she is involved in parenthood in a direct and unavoidable way. In the three months after the baby is born she is emotionally entangled with a new relationship involving dependence and responsibility in such a direct and immediate way that she may find it frightening.

The father is also emotionally affected in the early pregnancy months, on his own account as well as in response to what is happening to her. His feelings about fatherhood may be ambivalent, and almost certainly he will not have had, or felt the need to seek, opportunities to talk about fatherhood. His own father, his role model, may be a figure of admiration or worship, fear or indifference, present or absent, but powerful and usually unacknowledged. But it is stirred up by the new thought that he is going to be someone's father very soon. This is intensified after the baby is born — the reality of being a father comes home to him very strongly, and these first three months are as emotionally upsetting to him as to her.

It is astonishing how quickly the panic of actually having the baby fades into the past, for nearly all new parents. Once you have fed the baby successfully and it has fallen back to sleep, perhaps with your help in rocking or cuddling, you feel a lot better. And when 24 hours have gone by and you are still all three in good condition, you know that you are going to survive. You have surmounted the first hurdle, and although you know there are others ahead, you gradually feel you can get over those too.

Once a week has passed you look at the baby, and it has changed already. It has filled out, grown a bit. You know the sounds of its breathing and the expressions which chase across its face when it is asleep. You pick it up without difficulty or fear, and you are beginning to look for response and the first smile. You will survive, so will the baby, and your partnership looks promising and happy.

The baby's feelings

Throughout birth the baby is still getting food and oxygen straight into its blood system, through the placenta. Its lungs are full of fluid, but have been gently practising during the pregnancy when the rib cage muscles start working, getting ready for the job they will have to do after birth. Just before the baby emerges it is going through a tight squeeze, and its little rib cage is compressed. As it comes out, the pressure is suddenly removed, and the baby's chest expands, drawing air into its lungs. This is not the only influence which starts the baby breathing; there is shock at the feeling of cold air, and biochemical factors in its blood which stimulate it to start breathing, but the release of tightness round its chest certainly plays a part.

Starting to breathe is one of the immediate changes the baby experiences, but within its body all sorts of dramatic and important things are happening automatically. Valves in its blood vessels close to cut off the blood still pumping in from the placenta, and other valves open simultaneously so that the blood from the heart starts to flow round the lungs to be able to take up the exchange of oxygen and carbon dioxide. Its lungs take over the job the placenta has been doing up till then.

All in the same bewildering few minutes the baby has its first sight of bright light and shapes and colours, its first touch of cloth and skin, and probably soft rubber gloves. It has its first experience of hearing voices through air, its first experience of the influence of gravity, and its first smell of air, probably laced with antiseptic, and the warm rich human mother scents. It is no wonder that its automatic reaction to all of this is probably to cry out in surprise, and the very sound and feel of its first cry may astonish or frighten it, so that it continues to cry. Every adult in the room will be glad and reassured by the baby's first cry, but the baby itself may be in a complete spin of sensation and bewilderment.

Above all else, at that first moment away from its mother, a baby needs comfort and reassurance. That means warmth and a feeling of safety by being held close. Newborn mammals each have the strong instincts needed for their survival, and although newborn human babies never need to rely on them, they retain several of the instinctive abilities they share with other primates. They have the ability to feed, to hang on, to walk, to respond, and to learn.

At the moment of birth, and for a few hours after, these inborn reflexes are very strong. If you touch the palm of a baby's hand, it will grip your finger with a surprisingly strong grip. If you gently pull away, the baby will cling on tight, even sometimes to the point of being lifted up. If you hold a baby upright and allow its feet to touch a firm surface — without its weight pressing down on them — it will respond by placing one foot in front of the other as though it were trying to walk.

A newborn baby knows the sound of its mother's voice already, and left to itself it will turn towards her voice in preference to any other. If it has heard its father's voice throughout its life in the womb, it will turn to his voice rather than any other masculine voice. Another reflex it has is the habituation reflex which enables it to learn; if you clap your hands near to a baby it will jump with surprise, and maybe even cry if it is very sensitive to noise; if you clap again, it will jump a little less, and very soon it will have learnt that that sound, though sudden, is not followed by danger or disaster, and it will no longer jump when you clap your hands. It learns very fast to react to its environment and to sort out the unworrying sounds and feelings from the ones which make it feel definitely unsafe or insecure.

Perhaps most immediately important of all, a newborn baby can suck and swallow, and responds to a gentle touch on its cheek or lips by opening its mouth and trying to suck. Because of this it will often take to sucking at its mother's nipple quickly and easily in the hour after birth, and finds comfort and security in doing so. Some babies do not do this so readily, and find sleep is the best thing for them once firmly and warmly held by one of their parents. Usually it is the mother who holds the baby first after it is born, but if she has been delivered with the help of forceps, or by Caesarean section, it may be its father who holds the baby first of all.

Babies lose heat very quickly after they emerge from their mothers' bodies, so warmth is the first concern. It is delightful if they can be cuddled up close to the skin of their mother, and the two of them wrapped up warmly together in a big soft blanket.

After warmth, comes sleep, so that the baby can rest and recover from the exhausting business of being born. Babies are very peaceful in this time, and often they are not hungry; healthy babies will not die for lack of food for days after birth, and colostrum is all they need until about three days old. Given that they had a straightforward birth, without too many drugs, they will sleep a lot, and often wake quietly and just lie looking at the side of their cot and getting used to the new feelings and sensations.

These first days after birth are a good time for adjustment and reflection for all the actors in the recent drama of birth. The baby needs a peaceful time to get used to new feelings, inside and out. He or she has had so many strange experiences all at once, from being enclosed in soft cotton or wool clothes against the skin, to having cold air instead of very warm fluid in a mouth and chest which has so far only known steady blood heat.

Being picked up and carried swiftly in air must be as amazing as a first experience of flying is to any adult — that sensation of an enormous hand in the small of your back pushing you faster and faster ahead as the aircraft gathers speed down the runway, and then the sudden calm and lightness as contact with the ground is left behind and the aeroplane is free to climb steeply and churn up feelings of vertigo. People who fear flying find it very hard to relax into those sensations and trust the pilot absolutely; a baby can do nothing other than trust whoever picks it up. Its trust is absolute, and deserves some thought and understanding from the people who handle it. So many later reactions to experiences hark back to these early days of life.

So reassurance comes closely after warmth and rest for the newborn. Talk to your baby. It won't understand the words but it will learn the tones, and connect them with the feelings which go with them. Babies have been used to noise and movement of a swoopy rocking kind while inside their mothers and it is no wonder that adults holding them tend to croon and rock as a sort of automatic reaction to the feel of a baby held in their arms. Babies actually tell you what they need for reassurance, if you can watch and listen to their responses to whatever happens to them.

After a day or two the next feeling that the baby has to react to is hunger, which it has never known before, having been fed continuously while it was growing in the mother's body. It is arguable that a baby *in utero* in a starving mother may know what shortage of food is like; it is undoubtedly true that in the interests of the survival of the species, whatever nourishment is available within the mother's body, even if she is starving, will go to the baby, even if she suffers greater malnutrition as a result. In dire situations, like the concentration camps in Hitler's Germany, the babies of mothers starving under appalling conditions were reasonably plump, though small, when born; they didn't stay that way, being progressively starved after the birth, but while growing in the womb they got whatever was to be had.

Hunger is therefore a new sensation for days-old babies and must feel painful. Babies cry when they feel it. Anyone who has gone on a slimming diet at any time should be able to sympathise with a hungry baby; that hollow feeling which can grow into actual pain, and which you know can be quickly relieved by opening the mouth and eating some food. Your baby instinctively knows this too and will quickly respond to the offer of something to suck in its mouth, which produces milk — the food it needs.

The fascinating thing for a first-time mother is that her baby's hunger cry produces a strong physical reaction in her own body, which has nothing to do with her conscious mind. This can be a great surprise, and some mothers revel in the sensations, while others find them scary, and resist surrendering to the response. You can't tell until you have your first baby, and you need an open mind to be ready for anything.

Babies need sounds and movement. These are familiar already since the womb is a pretty noisy place. If you have ever put your ear on someone's stomach and heard the plumbing noises going on in that person's digestive system — all sorts of plops and wheezes and watery running sounds — you will know what kind and level of clamour the baby has been used to before being born. Add to that the steady thumping of its mother's heart above it which is always there, but sometimes gets faster, if she is distressed or taking exercise, and the in-and-out rushing sound of her breathing, and you realise that the baby is conditioned to hearing things going on all the time. It follows that complete silence is unfamiliar to a baby, and a cause of unease once the initial investigation of this new quiet is past. A baby does not need isolation or complete quiet to be able to sleep; indeed, those conditions may be the reason why it doesn't find it easy to sleep. You can almost imagine that the baby instinctively feels abandoned in this utter stillness and silence, and its cry has an element of 'Is there anybody out there?'

A newborn baby sleeps when its needs are met and it feels comfortable, wherever it is. Mothers who often carry their very tiny babies in a carrier on their front, know how easily the baby sleeps in the oddest positions, whatever is going on around it. As the baby grows to be too heavy for easy carrying in this way, it still likes to be in the centre of family activity, and will sleep when it needs, and watch and respond to all that is going on around it when it is awake.

Babies absorb rhythmic movement by the way they are handled from their earliest moments outside the womb. It is hard to think of a better example than the way that most African babies, carried on their mothers' back while she walks, or works, or dances, learn to move with grace and balance all their lives, and hand it on in the same way to their own children. Such children do not have to be taught to walk, run or dance gracefully, they know it all from earliest babyhood.

Warmth, rest, food, sounds, movement, all basic needs for the newborn. One thing more — a baby needs human response and contact. It makes overtures, initially by grasp and by trying to find something to suck, and crying for different reasons, and it needs a human response to these overtures. One of the most endearing things a baby does is to fall asleep on your shoulder as you hold it in your arms. The feeling of the utter trust that this little creature has placed in you by abandoning itself to the safety you have made it feel is something very moving. There's a two-way mutual reassurance going on which is deeply satisfying.

Babies in Special Care

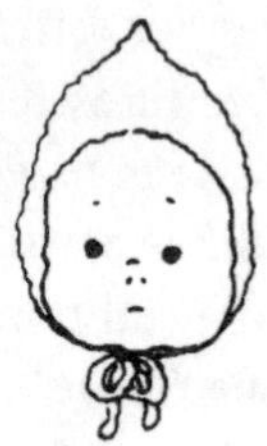

Sometimes, immediately after being born, a baby may have a problem and needs to be put in a Special Care Baby Unit (SCBU) at the hospital. This may be because the baby has been born earlier than its full term, and is premature, so that its development is not quite completed and it will have difficulty with breathing and feeding. It may be that during its development in the uterus some small detail has been bypassed — not because of any fault of the mother, but for some unknown reason — and the baby needs extra help after birth. Or it may be that the birth itself was complicated in some way and the baby has come under more stress than it can surmount without extra help from a forceps delivery or a Caesarean section. After such a birth the midwives and doctors monitor the baby's health and make sure that all is well by keeping the baby in conditions as near to those in the uterus — which it has just left — as possible.

Whatever the reason, having a baby put straight into Special Care inevitably poses special emotional problems for the mother and for the father. They may have been anticipating what they will feel when they see their baby for the first time; how wonderful it will be to hold their newborn child, and how relieved they will be to have the labour safely over and the baby a living, breathing reality. And now, without warning, the baby is whisked away after the briefest of sights, and the parents have more, rather than less, to worry about.

The sense of shock is very real. They have been expecting relief from the potential problems of late pregnancy and labour, and they have just been through hours of intense feeling, physically and emotionally, and now, immediately, they have a completely new and threatening situation to face. For the new mother, an assisted delivery also means problems of repair to her body, and pain from stitches in her vagina or abdomen. She will be denied the distraction of holding her baby while the stitching is being done.

For the father, the anxiety is numbing, for he has two to worry about now. If he has never heard of the possibility of a baby going into Special Care during whatever preparation he has been to during pregnancy, his bewilderment may be great. There seems to be no chance of asking questions now; everyone involved in a crisis is so busy and knows just what to do, and the father and mother simply have to wait until someone has time to explain fully to them what the panic is about in relation to their baby.

It is in this situation that the quality of care at your hospital is so important. The hospital comes into its own when there is any emergency, and a good hospital will include the parents as soon as possible in any decisions which have to be made. The mother and father need to know in full what difficulties the baby may be in, and why, and what the immediate future holds for the baby and for them. If they feel they are being kept in the dark and not told the whole truth, their distress and anxiety is greatly increased. Their worry may be unnecessarily great.

If a baby has to be in Special Care for longer than just a few hours, then the parents have a particularly hard time. A mother who is in hospital postnatally and who has to go to the Special Care Baby Unit whenever she wants to see her baby, feels very bereft compared to the other mothers in her ward. She may not even be able to hold her baby for some time, and this is a specially painful deprivation. Many hospital paediatricians now encourage parents to touch and stroke their babies who have to be in incubators, and teach mothers how to do this. This eases the anxiety for the mother, and helps the baby too. Mothers who have this experience say that the moment when the baby first comes out of an incubator and they can hold it is very special — almost as dramatic as a second birth.

Having a baby in Special Care may mean a longer stay in hospital. But the knowledge that the baby is in the best place may ease the frustration of not being able to go home as early as you hoped.

If the baby is in Special Care because he or she has been born prematurely, it may be that the mother has to go home alone, leaving her child in the SCBU until its ability to carry on life without extra help has developed. At this stage, she and the baby's father may feel specially deprived. They have a baby but it is not with them. Often they say that they don't feel like proper parents at all until the baby comes home. The mother, particularly, may feel bereft and at a loss, with unexpectedly nothing to do. She needs a lot of extra support.

If a mother with a baby in Special Care wants to breastfeed the baby, she will be encouraged to do so, especially if the baby is born a bit early. Mother's milk is the very best for the baby who has difficulties. She can express milk by hand — which some are very expert at doing and others find slow and frustrating. Or she can hire, or be supplied with, a milking machine or pump, specially designed to collect her milk so that it can be given to the baby. Many mothers in this situation have said that they felt so much better for being able to do something so vital for their babies as to provide milk for them, and that the work involved was worthwhile.

Having a baby with problems of any sort, short-lived or very serious, is always an agonizing worry. You are never sure which way the baby's life is going to go, and the baby looks so small and frail. You have to hold on to the knowledge that a baby clings to life tenaciously — and the endurance and courage of the newborn baby is astonishing. Babies *want* to live. They will try their best to keep going, and so will benefit to the fullest extent from all the help that is given to them. On some occasions the going is too rough for them, and they relinquish life. But if they can, they will take hold and you see that hold getting stronger and stronger each day.

Both the mother and the father need extra help and understanding support when all is not well with their newborn baby. They may have a lot to face together, and decisions to make. They will need trustworthy and wise people with whom to talk. So often, when friends hear that the baby is born with a difficulty, they do not know whether to visit the parents and talk to them, or what to say. So they decide to stay away. This can make the parents feel that they are isolated, or unwelcome, or even that they have done something wrong and should feel guilty! It is always worth making contact with parents in special distress; they may badly want to talk, to cry with a sympathetic person, and feel the care and kindness of other adults. If, on the other hand, they do not want to talk, they can say so. And any friend will know that the time for further help is not yet come, and will not mind.

Bringing a baby home from Special Care, after he or she has taken a firm grip on life and rallied from a shaky start is a moment of triumph. Parents feel a heady mixture of pride of achievement, for themselves as well as the baby. But they will also suffer a special terror at taking on the care from specialists. The mother may feel that the impetus for starting a new life with baby is not as strong as it would have been immediately after the birth; but the fact that she has had more time to get fit and firmly back on her feet, and been able to catch up on her sleep, is a decided plus. The anxiety over their baby will have enabled the parents to make several giant leaps in realizing the importance of parenting and the value of their baby.

Anti-climax and depression

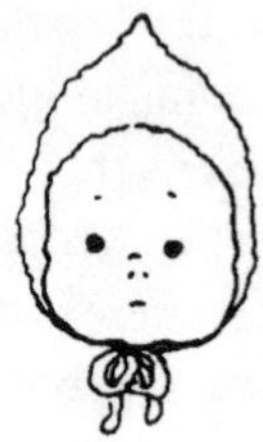

The birth of a baby is a life crisis, and like all other life crises it is necessarily followed by a period of adjustment and confusion. For most women, used to running their jobs and their lives efficiently, confusion is worrying. The balance of order is disturbed, and especially when a new person is part of the confusion it takes time to feel comfortable in a new routine. With a first baby the change is often so dramatic that it almost amounts to a culture shock! New parents say that however much they had tried to anticipate what life would be like when the baby arrived, they never had any idea that a tiny baby could fill their lives so completely.

Mothers vary greatly in their ability to adjust to the new demands on their time and energies. Some find motherhood interesting and absorbing, and, depending on the type of labour they have had, find their feet within a week or two — or three. Others take a month or more to feel that they have reorganized their days and nights satisfactorily. It is a great day when you first feel that you have control again and can plan ahead a little, instead of simply reacting to the baby's needs. It may not last for very long, but it's a comforting glimpse into a new era.

So much depends on the inborn personality of the baby, and your response to that child's needs. How you are physically after the birth — stitches or no stitches, drugs or no drugs, etc. — also matters. The first few weeks tend to be a damp time, since your emotions are being constantly stirred, and swing from delight to despair and back again with alarming speed, and tears are never very far from the surface. But it all begins to fall into place. Bit by bit, small achievements such as actually getting the washing done and some cooking ready for an evening meal, or the baby sleeping for a solid stretch during the day — or all through the night — reassure you that life is going to be containable, and fun, for you all as a family. The small achievements get bigger and more frequent and spirits lift and become more permanent.

'Third-day blues'

Most parents have heard about 'the third-day blues'. The majority of new mothers have some very good days immediately after the birth, and feel on an emotional high. The relief is so great that the labour which has occupied your thoughts for so many weeks is over and the baby is here at last. You feel physically lighter, even if you've had stitches, and the astonishing bulge of your stomach is gone. The baby is a wonder; the cards and flowers and congratulations come in, and there is help available if you need it. Hopefully the baby is a good sucker and you get help to establish breastfeeding so that the baby gets the essential colostrum. No wonder that life has a rosy glow.

But for some mothers this is not the picture they have experienced, especially if they have had a birth with difficulties, or if the baby is born with problems.

Whatever your initial feelings you may suddenly, apparently without warning, plunge to the depths. You begin to realize the responsibility of the baby's care, and how *totally* dependent on you this little creature is. You are suddenly aware that the birth, with its drama, is a thing of the past and that all the build-up of interest in your pregnant condition is a thing of the past too. You are now expected to get on with being a mother, and are apparently not nearly as interesting as you were when pregnant. You feel like the morning after the night before; the party's over, flat and dull. You also feel a bit hot and sweaty, not as well as you were the day before, and very tearful and unsure about anything that happens. Was this baby a good idea after all?

What is happening physically is that the milk production for the baby is getting under way. You have been producing colostrum throughout the pregnancy, but now, about three days postpartum, the milk is coming in and since this is an important job for your body, your temperature rises slightly and you are a bit feverish. Also your breasts get full and may be uncomfortable. The baby may find it harder to attach to such a full breast, and the peaceful feeding relationship is upset. Everything seems to be going wrong all of a sudden. It's at this time that you need very good help and support to learn how to ease the feeding technique. If you get that, the difficulties soon disappear. Without such help, this is the moment when so many mothers decide that breastfeeding is not for them — it's all too difficult, and painful, and humiliating.

Given supportive help and encouragement, this short period of blue feelings and inadequacy will soon pass — usually in about a week. The third-day blues are felt by most mothers, especially with their first baby. Many people today have heard about the horrors of postnatal depression, with the result that when new mothers greet their partner at hospital visiting time with floods of tears they may assume that they are inevitably in for full-blown depression. The father may assume the same and look gloomily at the future. But in fact his faith in things getting easier with time and practice, and his love and support of the mother in the first few days, are very good therapy indeed. They are a powerful help in the bounce back to confidence.

The third-day blues are *not* deep depression, but can deepen very quickly if the adjustment to the baby doesn't go easily. It is true that for many new mothers the first crisis of feeding when the milk comes in coincides with their return home from hospital, another moment of change. They may not have access to help, and may feel very alone so the visits from the midwife and health visitor are very welcome.

A new baby needs frequent feeding and a lot of attention, and this is always tiring until everyone gets used to it. Many people assume that the mother is suffering from postnatal depression when she is simply very tired and in need of another pair of hands to help with the extra work. It is at this time that help in the home is badly needed, and would often help prevent this depth of depression.

Puerperal psychosis

If, however, after a month, the chaos continues and the mother's tears and feelings of inability increase, then partners should be alert and watch carefully to see what is happening. If the baby is beginning to sleep well, but the mother is still unable to sleep, this could be a sign of overtiredness — or of depression. If the new mother is lethargic and increasingly unwilling to deal with the housework or tend the baby, it could be depression. If there is a noticeable change in her natural behaviour, from a liking for tidiness and order to a total disinterest in tidiness, or alternatively from a person who never notices mess to a person obsessed with everything being in meticulous order, this could be change of heart — but is far more likely to be a sign of depression. If a mother with a new baby loses all interest in eating, and is sick if she tries to eat, then there is something very wrong — and it could well be clinical depression. This is only suffered by one or two women in every thousand.

'Puerperal psychosis' can develop up to a year or more after the birth of a baby. It is beyond the control of the mother, being caused by a whole variety of physical and psychological factors. The onset of this depression may be slow, over a period of weeks, or may develop suddenly within a few days. Quick referral to the mother's doctor is necessary, and a refusal to underestimate the reality of this condition may need to be shown by the father. He will know, better than anyone else, how her state of mind has changed her behaviour, and how much she, and the baby, are at risk. Hospitalization may be necessary, though if possible the baby should be kept with the mother, especially if it is being breastfed. The links between the mother and her baby are very important in her recovery from this severe illness.

Severe puerperal psychosis is a rare occurrence, and *must* be treated by expert help. It can be short and sharp, or can take many months to get over. Predetermining causes are difficult to establish and appear to vary from case to case.

Long-continued depression

More common than one would wish is the depression which is long-continued but not acute enough to be obvious, so that partners and close friends fail to see what is developing. The new mother may be coping — just — but life with the new baby continues to be an effort for months. No joy breaks through, and relatives and friends become used to the mother feeling under par, and too frequently blame her for not enjoying her life. They either think she should make a bigger effort, or they lose interest and forget how she used to be. Joy seems to have left her life for good, and she may go to her doctor with a series of minor complaints — headache, backache, repeated pain after eating, or sickness — which do not respond to treatment.

When this happens, even the doctor may fail to connect her relatively minor ailments with postnatal depression; far too often she will end up on tranquillizers, because the doctor can think of nothing else to do for her. But tranquillizers are the worst thing to give her, since they do nothing but accentuate the flatness and lethargy she is already feeling, and may make her even more depressed at her inability to recover her spirits.

It is this long-continued, rather than acute, postnatal depression which is at last being recognized more accurately and addressed with more instant attention than it has been for many years. Whatever the reasons may be, such depression is more common than it used to be. For ten to fifteen per cent of new mothers it may last two months; for five to seven per cent it might continue for up to a year or even longer.

Causes of depression

There are several factors which affect the onset and development of these various levels of depression. Some are straightforwardly physical, some are emotional adjustments, and some are a rich mixture of both.

HORMONAL CHANGES

In the last few weeks of pregnancy the woman's placenta is making and releasing into her bloodstream a constant and rich supply of progesterone. This is the sex hormone which maintains the pregnancy and gives energy, and often a positive outlook, to any woman. The other sex hormone, oestrogen, which controls the onset of menstruation, is suppressed during pregnancy — for obvious reasons. The pregnant woman's health and peace of mind as she approaches birth is greatly dependent on the progesterone from the placenta.

When the placenta is delivered after the baby has been born, thereby completing the birth process, the supply of progesterone into the mother's bloodstream is suddenly cut off. It is estimated that in late pregnancy she is receiving 32 times the usual amount of progesterone from the placenta, and all at once this steady supply is no longer there. She has in her bloodstream a good supply which operates for some days, or weeks, but after that she receives no more at all until she starts to menstruate again, which may not be for many months after the birth — and this is unpredictable. Some women resume their menstrual cycle straight away, others not for six months or more. Breastfeeding appears to extend the time till resumption of menstruation, but is unreliable.

The effect of this sudden cut-off from the progesterone must always be felt by the mother, and the reaction varies from woman to woman, and is different for a woman with each birth. Much of the tiredness, the lassitude, the weepiness, and the effort of getting around to all the demands that need to be met postnatally is due to this shortage of progesterone in the mother's body. In days gone by this period of dramatic physical change was recognized as a time when women needed to be looked after, have lots of rest, and be well fed. No doubt this was often overdone, and the image of the Victorian mother, romantically adoring her sleeping child, but overweight and bored, has raised a strong reaction the other way, which has itself gone too far. Modern young mothers have virtually *no* rest time after giving birth before they are expected to pick up all their duties and responsibilities, plus the new baby.

BODILY CHANGES

Apart from the change in hormones, the woman's body takes some time to return to its pre-pregnant state. All her systems have been geared to making a baby, and now this task is completed her digestion and excretion, her breathing and sleep patterns, have to resume their job for her alone, rather than for her and the baby. Her muscles and blood vessels in stomach, back, legs and heart need to readjust. Her ligaments need to tighten up, and exercise is required to return her body to its earlier ways — and also to respond to new activities like carrying and bending to the baby, and pushing a pram or push chair. So physically getting back to — or on to — a new 'normal' takes time (see page 129), and is rarely taken into account in forward planning during pregnancy.

New mothers and fathers expect to be back to where they were before the pregnancy, and are surprised and daunted when this fails to happen. If the woman's body, for a variety of reasons, readjusts very slowly to its pre-pregnant state, this, when added to the sudden lack of progesterone, can cause severe clinical depression. In such cases swift medical help is needed.

LIFESTYLE CHANGES

The dramatic change in lifestyle is another reason for women to feel under a ton weight in the first weeks of a new baby's life. So often this is not expected, or allowed for, in the couple's planning ahead before the birth. If you have come from a large family you will have some memory of how the arrival of a new baby made life infinitely unpredictable for a while. But these days large families are rare, and it is very difficult to imagine the changes until you experience them, however hard other parents try to warn you, or you yourself try to plan ahead.

The woman of today, who works up to a month or two before giving birth, may enjoy the holiday feeling of freedom from office routine for a while, and many women say what joy they feel in being at home and building a family, rather than being at the beck and call of someone else. But others feel a great sense of loneliness with only a baby for company all day and every day, and miss the companionship of adults.

The complete change of routine may be difficult to come to terms with after a routine imposed by the firm for whom you used to work. A tiny baby is a very different sort of boss, and both parents may feel resentment in different ways over the restrictions on doing what you feel like when you feel like it. For example, you cannot go out for a meal or to a show at the last minute; now you have to plan for a baby-sitter, and maybe worry while you are away in case the baby-sitter doesn't look after your baby well. This can be very irksome, and you need to remind yourselves often of the long-term satisfactions which this baby will surely bring to your lives.

One way or another, you need to come to terms with any resentment, because otherwise it becomes easy to blame the baby for your depression, and the baby really doesn't want or need you to be depressed at all.

TIREDNESS

Tiredness is almost always a major cause of depression during life with a new baby. 'Is there life after birth?' parents wail, as they move through their days like zombies for lack of sleep. This time passes and, looking back, it is not long before the baby sleeps and settles down to life — but at the time it seems endless. In a strange way, this time of excessive tiredness proves to be valuable through the rest of your life — and not only because of the old analogy of banging your head against a wall because it's so nice when you stop. But the knowledge that you *can* survive such a time, and still be reasonably sane, and — even more important — that such times *do pass*, is a great strength when other times of stress, in work or relationships or illness, cause you to be under strain. Read the section on tiredness (page 107) for some ideas on how to combat it.

HOUSEHOLD PRESSURES

Another reason for the far too common experience of postnatal depression today is the strain on new parents of the domestic chores of daily living. It is important not to worry about everything being perfect. Lower your standards for a while. It will all come right in time.

It is unreasonable to expect a baby to settle into life away from its automatic existence inside its mother, until about three months after birth. Anything earlier than that is a terrific bonus — and is much more likely to happen if you have help with the day-to-day feeding, cleaning, shopping and washing routines, leaving you with more time and a less overloaded mind to concentrate on the baby and yourselves as parents. It is very unfortunate for *every* new mother, in whatever living conditions, that domestic service has such a bad and unjustified image in our country. If it were otherwise, so many dangers due to loneliness in the home, and over-strain, could be avoided.

A statutory Home Help service is still available in some areas and can be called on for maternity cases if your GP advises it. It would be of immeasurable benefit if some weeks of daily home help were to be routine for *every* parent immediately on coming home from hospital with a new baby. The arrival each day of a cheerful, practical person for three or four hours to share the chores and help you get used to the new needs of your domestic life makes such a big difference to your sense of insecurity.

OTHER CAUSES OF DEPRESSION

Other possible causes of postnatal depression include the environment we live in — chemicals in the drinking water supply, additives to food, sprays on vegetation, growth hormones fed to animals farmed for meat, preservatives in soft drinks, extra radiation, or gas release from industrial chemicals. All have been blamed, and no doubt all contribute to the general state of health or lack of health that we have to adapt to.

There is also growing awareness that more women and babies suffer from thrush than used to be the case. Thrush is caused by an organism (*Candida albicans*) which is a normal component of an adult's intestinal flora, but if it multiplies greatly it can affect other parts of the body and the results can cause depression. If a woman has thrush in her vagina when she gives birth, it is possible for the baby to be affected, and develop painful inflammation in his or her mouth. This makes sucking painful and the baby cries, so it is worth keeping an eye out for soreness or white spots in a crying baby's mouth, which might show that thrush is the cause. Women may be quite unaware that they have a high level of *Candida* in their bodies which is causing depressing side-effects. Men can be affected by high levels of *Candida* in their bodies also.

These factors may be the last straw in an age when pressures on parents have never been greater. Bringing up children and making a good job of it is expensive in time, energy and money. Conditions of work are often intensely competitive, and unemployment is high, so the anxiety level for parents is also a predisposing factor for depression if it strikes. I can only repeat that genuine understanding and helpful support are urgently needed for parents when every new baby is born.

Remedies

Practical help in adjusting to a new lifestyle must come at the top of your list of ways to avoid, or ease, postnatal depression. Choosing who to ask to help is important when trying to think beyond the birth of the baby. New parents who themselves have parents who are willing and able, non-judgemental and adaptable, are fortunate. Sometimes sisters or sisters-in-law are the best help, or friends. Sometimes a postnatal supporter is available from help organizations such as the National Childbirth Trust; but it might be just as wise to spend what money there is available on paid domestic help. If sleeplessness is an acute problem, you might arrange for someone reliable to take the baby for a walk in its pram every afternoon so that you can get your head down and sleep for a couple of hours. Such an arrangement can be a lifesaver in breaking a pattern which is putting a heavy burden on you.

It is all too easy to feel trapped in the house, especially in winter. If you begin to feel this way, put the baby in a carrier or a pram or push chair, and go out for a walk. It will not hurt the baby even in winter, if he or she is warmly wrapped up. And the fresh air will do you both good, even if it is wet or windy. Exercise is always refreshing.

Another trap for the unwary is to blame yourself for everything that is going wrong, such as the baby crying, the evening meal not cooked or the washing piling up. Try praising yourself instead! When the baby is bathed and dressed and the soup is made, pat yourself on the back. It may be a small job done, but it *is* done and *you* have done it, so praise is due. Small steps become big steps very quickly.

Some couples decide that extra help from relatives or outsiders is more difficult to cope with than handling the new situation on their own, and if this is the way they feel, they are more than likely to be used to sharing their thoughts and needs, and working together as a couple. Where this can be hard is if one parent has very definite views on the handling of a new baby, and the other parent disagrees totally. The last thing that one wants at this time of early adjustment is constant argument and recrimination.

The watchfulness of the father, who can usually be a bit more objective than the mother towards the newborn in the first week or two, is a wonderful help. He may be going through a very confusing time himself, so it can be asking a lot of him to set his own feelings aside and concentrate on what is happening to his partner and the baby.

For example, he may be longing to resume love-making, especially if it was a very important part of their relationship before the pregnancy, and also if he has found making love inhibiting during the pregnancy as she became larger and less active. He may have expected her to return very quickly to her enthusiasm and response to him, and be shattered to find that this doesn't happen. Her tenderness from stitches in the vagina, or bruising after forceps, her intense response to the baby due to anxiety and new responsibility, her milk-filled breasts which may overflow at any time, may all be very off-putting to him and make him wonder when, if ever, she will be a sexual partner again.

But if he understands what is happening and manages to make his partner grow in confidence about her handling of their baby and back her up in her learning about these new skills, then his rewards will be great. The mutual gratitude and appreciation between the two of them and their baby lays a sound foundation for their life as parents.

If depression does develop, either shortlived or longer and more serious, a new mother should never be blamed. She does not choose to be depressed; there are reasons why she feels this way, and there is always a way to help her and lift the depression. It's just finding it which can be confusing and difficult sometimes. Try practical help; try changes in handling the problems; try asking others who have gone through the same thing; try having a holiday, if that is possible. If the depression deepens, seek expert medical help without delay.

One point about hormone treatment, if that is suggested: if replacement hormones are advised and prescribed, only true progesterone will help, and progesterone cannot be given by mouth. It *must* be given by suppository or pessaries. British doctors are only gradually getting used to prescribing such treatments, which are used far more widely in other countries.

There are homoeopathic remedies which may help many women, and these can be tried without doctors' prescriptions. Evening primrose oil has a magical effect for some women, not only for easing depression, but for helping with premenstrual tension as well. A good chemist will have a stock of this, and be able to explain any other herbal remedies which might help.

On the subject of stitches, if they remain uncomfortable, go and see your doctor about it. No woman should endure discomfort for more than a month after the birth. It is very important to discuss any emotional or physical problems with your doctor at the six-week check-up.

The plus side

Depression at any time in your life need not be seen as an inevitable disaster, nor as an indication that you will be prone to being depressed for the rest of your life. Women who suffer from postnatal depression immediately feel guilty, even total failures, because women are used to being all-rounders. They want — and are expected — to achieve in all areas of their lives, and feel bad if they fail any of their commitments. Women have a marvellous talent for 'plate-spinning'. Particularly in family-building, it is often the mother who is keeping many different activities going at the same time — housework, husband, shopping, managing money, playing with small children, encouraging older children, helping with homework, welcoming friends and callers, dealing with children's friends and interests, and in their spare time going to the loo. When you see one plate beginning to flag and collapse, you rush to give it a twirl and get it spinning happily again. Fitting in your own career as well is often very hard, and feeling that you are not coping with it all, or fretting about being unable to fit your own job in after you have produced a baby, must inevitably lead to some depression.

Depression is a symptom. A sign that something in your life is not going right. Just as pain in your physical life points to something needing attention and makes you seek help and find out the cause, so depression and guilt should make you alert to some part of your life not being right, and needing change or improvement. Your reaction might be 'What am I doing wrong to be so down?' which is so often followed by guilt. More helpfully it could be 'What's going on here? What is making me feel so low? And what can be done about it?' It may be that there is little you can do about it at that particular time but endure; but equally there may be changes that are desirable and possible, if only in understanding *why* you are depressed and taking it on as something to be lived through.

The changes you find you need to make may be painful or difficult, just as treatments for physical ailments may be for a time. Acute onset of depression will need immediate professional treatment, just as a dislocated joint or an emergency appendix would do. But a gradual onset of depression is more like a gradually increasing stomach ache or backache which points to a need for change of diet or remedial help. The 'mind-ache' of depression calls for equal care in finding out the reason and doing something about it.

Another aspect of depression is that it means your mind is already seeking a cure for the problems. There's a parallel in the directly physical part of your life here too. If you cut your hand badly because a knife slips, you have immediate acute pain, bleeding, drama, and you may even have to get the cut stitched. Something has upset your body's balanced system. But after the immediate treatment for the cut hand, the healing process within your own body is actively at work — and it aches, and hurts, for quite a long time until it is completely better. Balance is restored and you gradually forget about it.

A similar effect occurs with the pain of depression. The conditions of your life which are causing the depression may be of the kind that can be immediately helped. For example, if you are anaemic after the baby's birth it can make you feel like death warmed up, which is infinitely depressing but can be treated effectively and quickly. Or the reasons may be ones that take more time to cure. For example, if you have a sick child, or a baby who does not sleep or a partner who hates his job, and you are very tired, then you are prone to depression and need external resources such as some sort of therapeutic help or friends to talk to, and inner resources, faith and strength to see you through the difficult time. But whatever the reasons, the depression means that your mind is already beavering away at a cure — the healing is happening.

Two useful organizations to contact are the Home-Start Consultancy and the Association for Post Natal Illness (addresses on page 191) both of which offer great support to women suffering this sort of depression.

Interview with Ella, who suffered very severe postnatal depression

Ella has two children. After the first son was born she found she had a baby who was acutely aware of noise, and couldn't sleep well for nearly two years. Since he woke at the slightest noise at night — the telephone, the door knocker, flushing the loo, or the sound of the television, she and her husband became increasingly isolated and shut in with their anxiety. The possibility that the baby had been affected by the unusually heavy drugging she had experienced in labour was never suggested to her, and the advice she had from health visitors and doctors was simply to endure the difficulties and he would sleep better in time. She feels strongly that it would have helped if she had known the possible reasons why her baby was so upset.

Until the baby was four years old, Ella was depressed and no-one seemed able to help. She assumed that the depression was caused by tiredness and loneliness. When it dawned on her that this might be untreated postnatal depression she sought further help, and found it from two sources: evening primrose oil, taken by mouth, and a course of progesterone treatment given by suppository or pessary. Both made a considerable difference, and she felt recovered enough after a year of treatment to embark on a second pregnancy, hoping that by having progesterone treatment immediately at the birth and after — initially by an injection — she would be able to avoid depression the second time.*

When she went into labour the hospital had not got the progesterone ready for her to have at the best time, so it was not until some hours after the birth that she got the injection on which she had pinned her hopes. For three weeks after the birth she felt fine, and thought she had avoided a repeat of postnatal depression. But then it gradually developed, and more severely than before. In her own words:

> 'I'd always wanted children, and always wanted to spend time with them, so getting postnatal depression was a shock. I felt guilty because I wasn't enjoying being a mum, when I'd wanted to be one so much. For the first six months after the second baby came I felt every day that having him was the biggest mistake of my life, and I said so to my husband over and over again. I never felt aggressive towards the baby, I just felt sorry for him, and I never let him hear me say that having him was a mistake. He's 22 months old now, and I wouldn't be without him for the world, I love him so much. I can look back now at the severe depression, but only for special reasons, like this interview. I've put it behind me now and I want to look forward, not back. I'm not going to have any more children — I've been sterilized — and I've felt a lot better knowing that. The threat of having to go through another bout of postnatal depression is gone.
>
> 'When my second baby was born, and they hadn't got the progesterone injection ready for me to have it at the birth and before the placenta was born, I was terribly upset. I'd read so much about it and I wanted to give it a real try, but nobody at the hospital really took it seriously; they just made me feel that I was a nuisance and obsessive, and why was I making such a fuss about this anyway? The injection was three hours late, and mentally that upset me badly. The labour had been very good, with good preparation this time, and I was so pleased with myself about that, and it just spoilt it to have to have

*Treatment recommended by Katerina Dalton in *Once a Month*, Fontana, 1978.

something going wrong when I was relying on other people.

'Nevertheless I got the injection after the wait, and then had more injections for ten days, as recommended, and for three weeks I felt fine, with lots of energy. I went on using suppositories, but the high progesterone affected my breastfeeding, and my milk supply went down, so I switched to low-dose suppositories, and continued breastfeeding, because I felt that the baby needed that more than I needed the progesterone. Looking back, I think that may have been a mistake — I might have stopped the breastfeeding and stayed on high-dose progesterone and who knows, might not have had such severe attacks.

'After eight or nine weeks the symptoms of depression started creeping in. I woke some days feeling weepy and very tired. None of the usual things that cheer me up helped at all. We live a long way from any town so I couldn't go out with the baby and look at shops or meet other mothers, and the weather was severe anyway. It got worse just before I started menstruating again, at six to seven months, and I got frightened because I started to do violent things. I got hypertension feelings, with buzzing inside my head. I'd try to control it, and then suddenly it would burst out and I'd find I'd hurled a cup across the room, or broken something else, and I'd burst into tears and lock myself in the bathroom and cry uncontrollably. The frustration would build and build inside me until it burst out. I pulled down a whole row of curtains once. I was amazed at my own behaviour — I felt like an onlooker watching someone else smashing cups and pulling down curtains. I'd cry all day some days, and I didn't dare go out, I looked so awful — I'd see myself in the mirror sometimes and think how dreadful I looked.

'My older boy was at school and I was so glad he was out of it. I'd somehow be all right by the time I fetched him in the afternoon. I badly needed to know someone else who had felt like this. I went to the doctor, and was referred to a psychiatrist who was working on alcoholism, and he confirmed that I had got postnatal depression, and not just what he called clinical depression. But he said he didn't deal with this specialized sort of depression. Unfortunately, there was no one within easy reach.

'I couldn't sleep, I had terrible nightmares. I couldn't eat, I'd look at food and just push the plate away. I lived on toast and tea. I went to see one of the gynaecologists back at the hospital, and he advised me to give up the breastfeeding. I loved breastfeeding the baby, I'd retreat into a cosy world of my own with the baby, warm and safe. I stopped feeding at seven months on the specialist's advice.

'I wanted a room of my own where I could escape from everyone — baby, child, husband. The locked bathroom was my refuge. The aggression was always taken out on *things*, not the baby, but once I found I'd hit the empty cot across the room, and that frightened me so much. After the aggression had burst out I'd be better for a day or two, and then it would build up again.

'I could put on an act. The only person I let into my life was one woman friend who would understand and lived near. I'd go along to see her sometimes and tell her how I felt. But I even restrained that because I was afraid of overstraining our friendship. I couldn't bother about food for the family. My husband did the shopping and cooked for himself and our older son.

'My husband's patience and understanding made it possible to live through it. If he'd been annoyed or irritable I'd have been in a mental hospital without any doubt. He gave me such practical help. But he couldn't talk about it with me, and I badly needed someone to tell me that I was not going out of my mind.

'Once I was back on the high-dose progesterone, after stopping feeding the baby, the violence disappeared gradually. I continued to have "down days", but not so many. I have mild down days before period time, when I'm normally snappy, but they're controllable, and I'm not in a terrible state.

I'm still dependent on progesterone, I know the violence is still underneath, and I need it from day nine or ten until menstruation starts, each month. It was ten months before I could find the energy to go out and join a mothers and toddlers group now and then.

'I lost all interest in sex while the depression was so severe. It was a long, long time, and my husband was super about it. It wasn't until after the sterilization that I began to enjoy sex in any way again.'

Q. Would living in a town have helped?
Ella 'It might have, but I can't tell. It was such a *shock*, having this happen to me. Maybe there would have been more contacts. I've been in touch lately with a woman in the town where the hospital is who has had it, but I could only talk to her on the phone, she was too far away to visit.'

Q. Would domestic help coming in each day have been helpful?
Ella 'Definitely yes! It would have been marvellous practical help, and eased the strain on my husband. Having another adult coming in to talk to and listen to would have been so good, and also it would have been a restraint on the crying and frustration, having an extra person there.'

Q. Is there anything more your husband could have done to help?
Ella 'Yes, I needed him to *talk* more. When he's worried he goes silent, and I'd hear my own voice going on and on. I needed to have response and interest from him in what I said and felt. I knew he cared — he was being so terrifically supportive — but I did so want him to *say* so.'

Q. Now that the postnatal depression is receding, is there anything you'd like to do now?
Ella 'Yes I'd like to be available to talk to anyone else who is

going through the same terrible experience. I know now what reassurance women need who have this, and it would be good to help someone else. It would make the bad experience worth while.'

Fathers' first reactions

Men think differently from women. In my own marriage I have wished a thousand times that I could immediately understand why my husband's reactions to people and events often differ so intrinsically from my own. It can't be put down easily to the differences in our upbringing, or temperaments, although these obviously play a part. The difference seems to be more fundamental, and I have welcomed the chance to exercise some lateral thinking, to move my mental position to a new angle, nearer to the one he holds. Very often the different viewpoints give a more accurate picture, round out the event or the person and make it three dimensional rather than flat.

When a baby has just been born, its father and mother share some emotions very strongly. Relief, for one, that the baby is out and breathing, and the labour is over. The birth may have been straightforward, or had some complications, but relief and thankfulness that it is at an end are always there. A deep sense of pride, too, at having completed the job of bringing a baby into the world is an expected emotion, always provided that the mother and the baby are doing well.

Many men, however, feel a sharp sense of isolation from their women at this time, because the woman has experienced a tremendous physical event and the man has been an observer, however closely identified he has been with the birth, and however wonderfully well he has supported and encouraged her during the crowded hours. Others feel profoundly grateful that this is one experience that they will never be asked to undertake.

Almost without exception, the men who have been present at the births of their babies, as active partners, are glad to have been involved. The 'feminine mystique' and awful unknown horrors of birth behind closed doors, with shrieks and groans feeding imaginations of awful torture and imminent death, have been done away with and replaced with the far less frightening reality.

The first very difficult moment in a new father's life comes quickly on the heels of the baby's birth. At that time of intense emotional involvement, when he is often overwhelmed with feelings that he has never had before, and has just seen his first child for the first time and hasn't yet absorbed the wonder of it, he has to leave his woman and his baby and go away, alone. He may be very tired, longing for sleep, or wanting a quiet time to absorb what he has just been through; he may be as high as a kite, on cloud nine, and wanting to shout and sing or dance round the ward, or celebrate his pride and joy; he may be hit between the eyes by the vulnerability of this tiny baby so real and warm and vocal, and want strong reassurance; he may be very much in need of close physical contact with his mate, to show her he loves and wants her and is moved by her giving birth, shaken by it all. But he has to go away and leave them, and return to an empty flat or house, often in the middle of the night.

This has never been brought home to me so clearly as when my own daughter had her first baby. Many husbands had spoken of the hardship of being alone just after the birth, and many had phoned their family or friends and found some relief in that. But it wasn't until I was with my son-in-law after the birth of that grandson that I realized to the full that it is not just company that a father wants after his baby has been born, but the *right* company, and that means the mother of the baby and the baby too.

Immediately after the baby was born the midwife and the doctor and myself were all intruders on his need. Leaving the ward was difficult, moving out of sight of his wife and baby cuddled up together on the delivery couch. He walked with unwilling feet down the long corridor, drove home in silence, and was like a bear with a sore head back at his home. Friends, parents, in-laws, relatives, he wanted none of them. All he wanted was to curl up in bed close to his wife and his baby, and talk over the birth they had just gone through, and share the exploration of this miraculous new little creature they had made and produced. He felt left out, excluded at a very important moment in their lives, and envious of *her* getting to know the baby when *he* was kept away from them. That may not have been what she wanted at just that moment, but it was what *he* wanted, and needed very badly.

Such a strong reaction is not universal, but if it was so for him, it is likely to be the same for many new fathers. Many express it in different ways. Asking a group of fathers what was the most difficult thing about the first few weeks after the baby was born I got the following responses:

Wes 'Anxiety after they came home from hospital until I was sure the baby was all right and well, and that we were doing the right things. We were such very new parents and had had nothing to do with young babies. Once some sort of routine was worked out and the baby was doing all right in our handling it was easy.'

Ian 'Being away at weekends so often because of my job. I hated missing those times with the baby. She was so good and slept well and grew so fast.'

Mick, after much thought. 'Oh, the out-laws, I suppose. There were so many people around, and I just wanted to be alone with Linnie and the baby. Those are such precious days and they go very fast. There's not much you can do physically. I mean, you can't feed the baby — that's all done by her. But

I needed to be close and cuddle him, and I could support them all through, only there were always people getting in the way. Very loving, helpful people, but if we had another baby I'd get rid of all the relatives if I could, and just have domestic help which came and went.'

Bernie 'Being away so much, working offshore on the rigs. I couldn't do much to help, or get to know the baby in the early days. I missed that.'

In the general discussion not one of them mentioned sleepless nights or crying babies, and all were enthusiastic about tiny babies and their pleasure in watching them and holding them, and seeing the speed with which they learn and grow.

I asked them why it was that they were so positive about these traditionally difficult days, and why the mess and muddle of early babyhood appeared to be insignificant to them. They talked about this and suggested that it might be because all of them were in jobs which required a good deal of self-reliance and independence; some were married, some were not but were in stable relationships, and each couple had *chosen* to have their baby.

It seems that independent-mindedness is a positive help in making the most of new parenthood. If both parents are used to trusting each other in times when they are apart, appreciate each one's ability to cope with life, and never seem to have as much time together as they would like, then shared decisions are easier to make, and mutual appreciation seems to be more readily expressed.

New babies do take up a lot of time, and some men are not prepared for the reorganization of life at home which follows a birth. For the first days and weeks it seems as though the baby is either needing to be fed, feeding, or coping with its digestion after feeding.

It helps to understand that a small creature which has been fed automatically through its blood system for all its life till birth will want to feed often during its first days out of the mother. Demand feeding is now widely understood and encouraged, and babies vary considerably over how quickly they settle down to any sort of routine after they instinctively learn how and where to get the milk they want.

But some fathers have very definite views about breastfeeding, strongly for or against, which may reflect their own parents' experience of feeding their children. Now that the importance of breastfeeding has been re-established, it is also sometimes hard for a woman to reconcile the needs of the baby with the needs of her career. Men have views about the issues involved too.

Once again it is important that there is mutual appreciation of each partner's feelings, and that dilemmas are talked about and decisions made which give the woman the most peace of mind. In the first few weeks the baby is so very much *her* dependant, and everything goes better then and later if she is happy about the way she feeds the baby. She will not be content at all if the baby's father disagrees with the methods she chooses.

Fathers also seem often to have quite strong views on the need for discipline in children. Very young babies do not take kindly to rigid discipline, and there are few things more wearing than trying to impose a routine on a baby who is not yet ready for it. Given help and warm understanding of its needs in the very early days, a baby very soon learns to feel secure, and most will fall in with a flexible routine within a very few weeks. But if a pattern of fighting the baby is established, it will feel insecure and will demand attention stridently and with distress to all concerned.

Babies will frequently settle to sleep better when rocked and carried by their fathers than by their mothers. There are several reasons for this. Men hold babies firmly, and babies like the security this gives them. Men have deep, slow voices, and babies prefer the lower registers of the human voice in their first few days and weeks. Men smell different from women, and if a baby is being breastfed its mother smells deliciously of warm food and is exciting as a result — often not sleep-inducing at all. It can be very flattering to a new father to find that he is the preferred comforter to his baby. Also on a more practical level, I know one young mother who says her baby girl much prefers to cuddle up to her father in bed after being fed, because of his hairy chest which is so soft and warm. He says he doesn't mind in the least being made to stay in bed because the baby has such a tight hold on his chest hairs that it's painful to disentangle the tiny fingers!

Emotions can be mixed immediately after the baby's birth, and much depends on the relationship between the parents. Fathers may feel the same sudden rush of caring warmth for the baby that so many mothers experience, and in our society, with its peculiar stiff-upper-lip attitude that requires men to act 'macho', fathers may feel embarrassment when this hits them or not know how to express what they feel. Emotion bottled up is difficult to deal with, and this tenderness for the very young and helpless is such a valuable basis for fatherhood that it really should find expression from the start. The lucky men are those who can ignore their surroundings and all other people, and give full rein to their feelings for the baby and its mother there and then. In many hospitals now, the parents are given plenty of time alone with their baby immediately after the birth, once the baby's condition has been checked and before the mother and baby are transferred to the postnatal ward. Many parents speak afterwards with joy of that time together, when their minds and hearts are most full of immediate reactions to the baby's arrival.

It is interesting to know what parents who are freed from the inhibitions of onlookers do at this time. A paediatrician* has done some research into this, with the parents' consent, and has filmed this quiet time of peace after the birth with a hidden camera. The baby has been wrapped up in cloths and shawls and given to the mother in bed, with the father there too. Without exception, when left alone the mother unwrapped the baby and stroked and kissed its head and arms and legs and body, the father joining in too with his arms around them both. Fingers, toes, ears, hair, all touched with loving care and great interest, before the baby is cuddled up close to the mother, often with just skin to skin contact, and both mother and baby wrapped up together in warm blankets. Immediate reassurance for the whole family is instinctively supplied by such

*Aidan Macfarlane at the Paediatric Department, Nuffield Hospital, Oxford.

a physical expression of concern and loving kindness.

However, if a new father is very dependent on his partner for reassurance for himself before the baby is born, he may initially react against her absorption with the baby, and feel excluded. He may not have thought ahead and anticipated that she will feel an immediate weight of responsibility and will turn to him for reassurance. She has moved on a stage and wants him to move on with her. In a way, she needs him to play the role of father to *her* while she finds her feet as a mother, and this is a valuable practice for the relationship he is entering into with the baby. Her need for dependence doesn't last very long — she will be back to her competent self within weeks — but it can be a time of stress for him if he has never expected such a development. A moment of stress is always a moment of opportunity too, and his response to this one is important to their future as parents.

On the other hand, if he has thought this out beforehand and is expecting her to need his help — practically and emotionally — and his reassurance that she is a good mother, and then she sails ahead quite competently into motherhood and finds great fulfilment with the baby, he may feel very disappointed, as though his careful planning had been spurned. This can be hard to understand.

I remember well a new father who gave great interest and support to his wife during pregnancy, and was eager to be with her in labour and to support her through it. She thought that this was what she wanted too, but when she reached the birth she suddenly found that, given the choice, she would have preferred to give birth on her own in a quiet dark corner, just like a cat. *Any* attendants were a strain for her. She could just tolerate the midwife, who she knew was necessary in case anything went wrong, but she didn't want her husband near her at all. This he found very hard to take, after all his thinking ahead and preparation for this drama. It was to his eternal credit that he accepted her complete change of outlook, and his own disappointment, and had no recriminations afterwards. One interesting follow-on to this was that for her second birth she wanted him there all the way through! Such is the unpredictability and individuality of each birth.

The most important thing is to keep an open mind, and be prepared for anything in the way of emotional response to the arrival of the newborn. It's a mistake to believe that parents bring up children — the reverse is often more true. Babies start the upbringing of their parents by making them learn something new about themselves. This brings people to a new sense of humility. That something so small and with so short a hold on life can make you feel so profoundly one way or another is amazing to many men. But it would be a great deal more worrying if a father had absolutely no emotional reaction to the new life he has created. That would indeed give cause for concern.

Interview with John and Diana

John said that having his own children gave him a sense of completion. Becoming a father gave a point to his life. He had a happy childhood himself, and looks back on it as a wonderful upbringing in inner London. He remembers being sent away when his younger brother was born, and feeling pushed out. He resented the new baby, but the brothers became, and have continued to be, good friends. When his mother died, his father took over the dual role of both parents, and did it very well in John's estimation. He has no criticisms of his parents.

Diana is an only child of older parents. She was sent to private school, made few friends, and was quite lonely. She looks back on childhood as a time of moderate happiness. She feels she was a late developer, and grew up suddenly at seventeen. She met John, and they lived together for a long time and travelled widely before deciding that they wanted to start a family.

John said that when Diana first became pregnant he was delighted and over the moon. At the same time he became worried on two counts. He worried that he had little experience or understanding of young children. His second, most urgent worry was about the possible damage the birth could do to Diana and the baby. He really needed help from the antenatal classes they attended and still uses the breathing techniques they were taught if he finds himself suffering from any sort of stress.

Diana hadn't wanted children, and worried about bringing children into a world so full of bad things and horrors. Once pregnant — accidentally — she knew it was the right thing. She bloomed in pregnancy.

> **John** 'I shall never forget the birth of our first daughter, Willow. It was the most exciting thing of my life. Just after she was born I became unemployed, and was able to spend a lot of time with her. I enjoy children, and want to spend more time with them than I can. I often come home from work ill-tempered, and I regret being impatient or easily cross with them. I'd like more time to play with them.
>
> 'Our children have destroyed a lot of sacred cows for me. They are so appreciative. I try not to push my interests on them because I'm very sensitive about kids' development. I'm slightly apprehensive about the teenage years, which will come very soon. I'm very keen on respect, and I think a lot about what wins respect from children. I think freedom comes with moral values.
>
> 'Di and I don't have enough time together. We're both tired in the evenings. We have five children now and this Council house is small, so we have very little privacy. Di minds this more than I do, because I spend evenings every week away at the club. Di finds this unfair, and resents it a bit. I am anti Women's Lib — I think that's unfair, because men can't do the opposite.'

Diana loves having the children, and has found them very fulfilling even though she had no previous experience of family life. She doesn't think John has the slightest idea of what motherhood involves. He loves the children and thinks about them a great deal, but he can't put up with them all the time — and doesn't have to since he goes out to work. He also insists on going out several evenings a week to his club. He cannot see that she has the same needs for time of her own away from the home which they both love. He seems to share the basic male belief that being a housewife and mother is not a 'job', for all his exceptional sensitivity to the role of fatherhood, his support at the births, and his love for babies.

> **Diana** 'It's a bit academic for him. He *thinks* about it, but putting parenthood into practice is another thing. The hour-by-hour, day-to-day caring for young children would drive him round the bend. He thinks that housewives/mothers are "free" and Women's Lib is greedy and unnecessary. I wish men could do some lateral thinking and see the soft and clinging chains of loving and caring for children. I hate one's own beloved babies being a bone of contention between their parents, for lack of generous understanding. But I do need time away from home as much as he does.'

Diana, like many other women, wonders if pay for housewives would up-grade the job in men's eyes, and if that is the only way to make fathers realize how hard mothers with babies work.

Interview with Matt and Christine

Matt grew up in a small family in the north of England, went to university in the south and has a job which keeps him in the south. His parents have found being grandparents very difficult to adjust to, and resent Matt's separation from his roots.

Christine grew up in a large family, with a father who travelled abroad a great deal and was often absent in her early years. When she reached her teens his job kept him more at home, and she and her brother and sisters have a strong friendship with him which is very valuable. She always found arguments and crosscurrents within her family hard to bear, and avoids ill-feeling as much as she can. She has found her in-laws' lack of interest in her and the children extremely hurtful.

Matt felt being involved in the labour was a good thing. There were no preparation classes anywhere near the rural town in which they lived when their first child was on the way. Christine worked at the Job Centre throughout her pregnancy; on two separate occasions their small house was burgled while she was at work, and this made her very nervous. Matt was glad to have been present at the birth and would have hated to have been excluded. He would have felt short-changed, and he can't understand men who won't be there; he knows how much support women need in a hospital.

The birth was in a small hospital in a provincial town. In the event it was wonderful, largely owing to the single midwife who was on duty and was superb. He had a small feeling that everything to do with the birth was geared towards the baby's wellbeing, and that the mother was excluded. After the birth Matt was 'unexpectedly knackered' and felt a sense of awful deprivation. It suddenly dawned on him that a third person was there, and that he and Christine would never be alone together again.

Matt 'I'm very glad I was there. I felt deeply involved in the first stage, when I could help Christine with her breathing, holding her and massaging her back when she wanted it. But in the second stage it was not so good; Chris had some drugs and she retired into herself with the intensity of feeling, and I couldn't help her as much as I'd like to have been able to. I hated leaving her behind in the hospital — I wanted to have her and the baby to myself. In a way I resented the baby, and wanted to discipline it so that it didn't spoil our life together. I suddenly realized how helpless and totally reliant on us this new little person was. Responsibility weighs heavy; when you get married, your wife is only partially dependent — you feel she *can* cope when you are away. But this little thing couldn't. I suddenly saw that we would never be able to make any spur-of-the-moment decisions again. However much preparation a man gets in pregnancy, the arrival of the baby is still a step change.'

Matt went on to say that when the baby came home with Christine he was afraid to be left alone with it. He had never had anything to do with babies or young children and had spent all his adult life with other adults. When the baby could crawl and respond, everything changed. Smiling was great, but when he tried to talk, and to follow Matt when he moved away, then he was hooked.

Christine found the hardest thing to cope with after the baby was born was deprivation of sleep. She couldn't get a proper sleep in hospital, and when she came home to her own bed a long sleep was the greatest essential. Sleeplessness during the first few months was by far the most difficult aspect for her.

As the baby grew, she noticed that many of her friends' husbands 'did a hell of a lot for their wives'. Hers didn't, and she resented it! Once the baby was crawling and talking the resentment lessened, and they now find life much less restricted than they feared, and a great deal richer for the baby's presence. They can't imagine life without him. But it took time for them both to settle down and see the joys of becoming parents.

Overcoming the problems

It may be difficult for some men, especially very young husbands and fathers, to understand what can be a dramatic change in their partners after they have given birth. Whatever course the labour may take, giving birth is a vivid physical experience which alters a woman's perception of her own body. She is subtly changed by the feelings she has gone through, and the sensations, the effort, and sometimes the sheer hard work and endurance she has had to summon up over many hours. Out of it all she has produced a baby, and her reaction to the child of her body is intense. She may be frightened by the intensity — either for or against the experience of the last few hours — or elated by it. She may feel something in between these two extremes. She is without doubt affected by it, and has gone through a rite of passage between one state of being and another. Women who adopt a baby go through the same experience but in a different way, somewhat slower and more bewildering, without the inbuilt reactions to the physical stresses of labour. But all women with their first new baby find their minds are concentrated on the infant, whether they want that absorption or not. Their child cannot be ignored.

As the father has not had the physical experience, he is not inevitably forced into this quantum leap of feeling like a father. He may instead feel that his mate has withdrawn from him, or at least has withdrawn her interest from him. He may feel jealous of his own child, because the baby seems to have come between him and her.

In the first few weeks he may resent the fact that no matter how interesting the thing he is saying to her, or the activity they are engaged in together, if the baby wakes and cries, or gurgles and smiles, her attention is immediately diverted to the baby. This even extends to love-making. Every parent can remember the instant frustration of the baby waking and giving a cry just as they are relaxed and absorbed in making love. It is laughable when you look back on it, but it's not always so funny at the time, especially for the father, whose response to the baby is not innately programmed. He may have been looking forward to uninhibited love-making for a long time, and feel irritation or resentment toward the third party who is now inhabiting the same house, even though he has made the third party himself. He may find it hard to accept that he is no longer the only person his wife loves.

Men may also find it hard to come to terms with the length of time that is sometimes needed for a woman's body to recover after giving birth and be ready for active love-making again. The passage of a baby through her vagina causes some bruising, depending on variables such as the size of the baby and the quality of the elasticity of her particular tissues. The bruising can be very much reduced by the use of Arnica, an old-fashioned herbal remedy taken by mouth at the very beginning of labour and applied as an ointment after the birth is completed. If she does not know about this, a new mother may feel very tender for many days after the birth, and it takes a good six weeks for uterus and vagina to settle back to their normal state. Stitches may complicate and increase her discomfort, and are a perfect nuisance to many women. Equally they can be a source of great frustration to many men, particularly if they fail to realize how painful the stitches can be. A little exercise of the imagination helps. If a father can imagine how he would feel about making love after he had had his penis slit and stitched up again, his understanding and sympathy for his wife's reluctance would increase.

A man's emotional reaction to being at the labour may also make a resumption of love-making difficult for him. If he has supported his partner through her labour and has helped her to breathe and relax and endure sometimes quite considerable pain, he may have said to himself that he never wants to see her go through that experience again — even though within a few minutes or hours after the birth she is bright and glowing and may even be talking about how she will change things in her next birth! He may then feel inhibited about making love to her and risking another pregnancy.

His emotional turmoil about any future births may be greatly increased if he has been watching from the midwife's end of the bed, and has seen the episiotomy. This sight can stick in a man's mind and be a source of anxiety for a long while afterwards.

In my experience, most fathers are happier when they are encouraging and helping the birth at the head end of the mother — it is her mind and her emotions which get neglected when the midwife and doctor are busy with the actual emergence of the baby. That said, I think of so very many fathers who *have* spoken with wonder about watching their baby emerge.

Since there are so many negative emotions possible when a man becomes a father — such as rejection and envy, jealousy and insecurity — and most of all the cultural restrictions on men showing their emotions, it is crucial that men who are about to be fathers have the opportunity to go to groups where these matters can be talked about and thought about. Classes for preparation for childbirth are widely available in Britain, but not all accept the fathers as an integral part of the group. Provision is usually made for one 'Fathers' Evening', when information about the course of labour, the most commonly used drugs and hospital procedure is given. Sometimes a film of birth is shown, and since the quality of these films is very variable, the value of them as a preparation for the unique birth he is going to experience is debatable. Such classes are really preparing men to be useful labour companions and no trouble in hospitals.

Really good classes give time for the discussion of all aspects of the approaching change of status for both women and men. (See page 191.) Men and women can be reassured when they find that other couples share their interests and their bewilderment. These classes can be great fun and release a lot of tension and anxiety. The couples who attend them come from all walks of life, so the men encounter new outlooks, angles and experience, and both parents are free to be themselves without any inhibitions of family or workplace. The class can become your own support group, and can lead to friendships, sharing of experience and help after the babies are born.

The birth of a first baby is a crisis stress time in the relationship between a man and a woman, and it is often blamed for the breakdown of a marriage. Too many marriages come apart during the first year of parenthood. Thinking ahead during pregnancy can make all the difference, and replace the disappointment, frustration and inarticulate anger which may make a man feel like walking out on his new family — or a woman weep over the baby, convinced that she is unsupported and unloved in her motherhood. With any luck your sense of perspective will not desert you, and you will know that the short-term difficulties will soon be compensated by the interest and reward of seeing your child grow and develop.

It is the understanding and kindness of man to woman and woman to man, and both to the baby, which are the foundation stones for building a family. Given these two, you should grow together and not apart when your first child is born. You may be sorry that one phase of your life is now in the past. You may feel the occasional twinge of regret that personal time and space now has a very different meaning. You may wonder why you feel that a whirlwind has hit you since that birth-day. But you now have a stake in the future. You three are part of each other. You have each gone through a big experience and the meaning of life for each of you is tied up in the other two. It's a profoundly exciting trio to be part of.

NEW MOTHERHOOD

Introduction

The birth of your first baby marks the end of your self-centred life. That is a statement of fact rather than a criticism of self-centredness. When you give birth to the baby you are no longer one alone, or two alone; you are part of a trio. The baby is a new individual, but you have created it, during 40 intensive weeks, from a single cell to the warm breathing bundle now in your arms. Your reaction to your daughter or son may be ambivalent, or fearful, or amazed, or all joy, or all fear, but there is no denying that you *have* a reaction, and whatever the course of your mothering — and your fathering — the bond between the baby and you is a permanence in your life from now on.

Mother and baby are in a very real sense two in one. 'You in me — you and me' as the caption on one photograph in a book says. Whatever affects the mother affects her baby, and whatever the baby does or feels affects the mother. The closeness and response may feel uncanny at first. If the baby is calm and sleeping well and sucking strongly the mother feels reassured and successful; if the baby is distressed and uncomfortable the mother feels concerned and unsure. On the other hand if you are feeling cooped-up and are fretting to be free, your baby will sense your unease and be jumpy and clinging; if you are fulfilled and contented the baby is more likely to settle to life without unnecessary distress. Whenever one or the other of you is having a problem it can be extraordinarily difficult to decide which of you is the cause!

The very closeness of the relationship can feel frightening at first. Babies are such a surprise to so many mothers; you know about them in theory, you have seen — and admired or disliked — other people's babies, but your own is quite a different matter. *Babies are not lumps of plasticine, to be pressed into the mould of your choice; nor are they objects to be enjoyed, or used, or abused for your convenience. They are small children, with a future which is in your hands. You can make their life heaven or hell, by your own choice* — and a baby can do nothing about it except react to his or her feelings. A baby does tell you what feelings and problems she or he has, but not in adult talk. You need to learn a new language which has more to do with observation and intuition than anything else.

If you watch mothers and small children in the street you can see many examples of this. A toddler will cry and reach up his arms to be picked up, and if the parent does not respond may be dragged along by the hand crying or screaming. Often this is more strain than the parent can stand and the child is punished for the upset being caused. But if the parent would just get down on hands and knees and see what the street looks like from the child's level, what would they see? A forest of knees and shopping bags and umbrellas and briefcases coming from all angles at the level of the child's head and eyes, so that the little one is dodging and flinching all the time — and cannot even see where it's going. No wonder the child asks to be picked up!

Seeing life as much as possible from the baby's point of view is a tremendous help in making sense of the early weeks and months of a child's life, and starts a habit of understanding which makes for better mutual relationships in the years ahead. It helps to avoid mothers blaming themselves for everything that is not quite perfect in the first months of babyhood. It also helps mothers to learn gradually to trust their instincts about the new baby. Even if it is your first baby and you have never had anything to do with babies before, you have strong inborn knowledge about the handling that your particular baby needs. But it is sometimes very difficult to trust this, particularly if your instinctive feeling differs from advice you have been given. So sorting out your priorities in your new partnership with the baby is intriguing, for both mother and father.

Crying

A baby's only way of communicating vocally is to cry. Since mothers are biologically 'programmed' to respond to their baby's crying, a fruitful means of getting to know each other is set up already when the baby is born. The burden of understanding is heavily on the mother's side, and most new mothers find this interpretation very hard at first. If they cannot quickly soothe the baby, anxiety grows, together with a feeling of frustration and inadequacy. Confidence is in very short supply, especially if the new mother has had little to do with babies in her life up till now. This is a much more common situation now than it used to be since families are smaller than a couple of generations ago.

Most women are unprepared for their physical and mental response to their newborn babies. The sound of your baby crying immediately produces strange feelings in your solar plexus, as though there was an invisible silken cord stretched between you and the baby, tugging at you. There is a physical response in your breasts too, whether you are establishing breastfeeding or not; they may feel tingling up near the armpits, and milk starts to leak from your nipples. Obviously the baby's need for nourishing is expressed by crying and its mother is being told *by her body* what to do. It is this which sometimes feels strange and frightening if you are used to deciding on your actions mentally, and making decisions independently. Suddenly you are being told what to do in a quite different way, by baby-led physical responses within yourself. It is almost a new experience.

Almost, because you have already known how to be prompted by your body in your responses to sexual experience, and this can have a profound influence. If you have found sexual response difficult, or painful, or have known unhappy contexts for the conception of your baby, you may draw back instinctively from another strong response in the same areas of your body. Since the baby is part of your sexual life it is not surprising that the sexual connections are there. If, on the other hand, you have enjoyed your sexual loving very much, you may find it disturbing to find a strong physical reaction to the cry of a baby! The context seems so different, and you may not have made the connection between conception and birth. Sex, after all, is a very clever and successful means of reproduction, evolved to ensure that human beings survive as a species.

This physical response to a baby's crying extends often to hearing *any* baby crying, not just your own. Every mother knows how hearing a baby in a pram in a supermarket alerts you at once, and you may have to be stern with yourself to avoid going to pick it up and soothe it. There's a sort of universal motherly attitude which comes with having your own baby. A woman told me that one night in hospital, after her first baby had been born a few days before, she woke and heard her baby crying in the nursery. In that hospital it was the rule that babies were removed from the ward to the nursery at night, so that mothers could sleep without interruption. She lay and waited for someone to go to her baby; no one did. The baby's crying grew more insistent, and then frantic, and at last she could stand it no longer. She got up, tiptoed down the ward, where everyone else appeared to be fast asleep, looked in the midwives' room and could find no one, and so opened the nursery door and went in. She lifted her baby, soothed it and fed it, and it dropped asleep in her arms; so she tucked it up in the cot, tiptoed back down the ward, got into bed, and just before she dropped off to sleep she suddenly thought 'I suppose it *was* my baby?'! She had not even read the label on the cot in the half-dark, and had simply responded to her strong instinct to come to the aid of crying babyhood.

It is this overwhelming instinct of response to a baby which not only makes many women draw back in fright when they first feel it, but equally makes it so desperately hard if the baby is stillborn or handicapped so that it may die soon after birth. The emptiness when you feel the physical answer to hearing any baby cry is real torture, and you need loving support and the chance to grieve for a very long time. We have all read of babies being stolen by women in this situation, and often it is not until you have your own first baby that you can begin to know how this can happen, and feel compassion rather than censure, for the stealer as well as the desperately worried mother and father whose baby has been stolen.

The baby is not consciously aware of the effect that his crying has on you. The baby has only one way of saying 'I am too hot', 'I am feeling very cold', 'I am hungry', 'I have eaten too much and want to be sick', 'I want to turn over please', 'My nappy is too tight', 'I'm all alone and don't know where I am', 'I'm lonely', 'I've just heard a horrid noise/felt a horrid feeling and I don't know what it was — help me', 'I *need* you', or 'I don't really know what the matter is but I want someone who smells and feels and sounds like Mum or Dad' — and that is to cry! A baby can only have utter trust that there is someone out there who will respond to the cry.

If you have never had the chance to handle and cuddle a baby, it feels awkward at first, and most new parents are scared of dropping their baby. This is a good feeling, since it results in the baby being held really firmly, which babies like and need. They are used to firm holding, which they have had all the time in the womb, and they find air very scary. If you put a newborn baby down on its back on a flat surface, with nothing — such as a blanket — round it, it rolls about and snatches outwards with its arms, feeling desperately insecure, and screams with fright. That cry is different from the cry of hunger, there's a note of panic in it, to which the parental response is very quick action. It is usual now to teach new mothers to change the baby's nappy on a changing mat, with the baby lying flat; experienced mothers and midwives always tuck something warm down each side of the newborn baby to make it feel secure in this strange position, so that it does not roll from side to side. They also talk to the baby all the time they are changing the nappy, so that nappy-changing becomes good fun from the start.

Since crying raises such anxiety and distress in a new mother, it is worth learning how to soothe and reassure your baby as soon as possible. This is much easier to do in your own home, as anyone who has managed to have a home confinement will agree. In hospital you always feel under observation, and wonder if you are doing it 'right'. Comparisons with the way other mothers and midwives handle babies are always in front of your eyes, and it takes great courage to handle your baby in any way differently from everyone else. At home you just work out your own way from the start, with advice from the visiting midwife.

Babies are not stupid, nor are they malicious. They do not cry to annoy you, or test you out, or spoil your life! They cry because they have a need and in the first early days their needs are to do with sensations. They feel lack of safe support and that is a cry of fear. They feel strange and new sensations like breathing and seeing and hearing and touching and that is a cry of surprise. They feel the workings of their bodies, digesting and peeing and passing a motion and that is a cry of mixed content — surprise to start with, and then first experiences of pain. No adult who has known heartburn will be surprised that a baby finds digestive wind in the stomach or bowel painful, and also what exquisite relief the baby has when it manages to burp or fart. They feel loneliness and that is a cry of appeal. All their cries are asking for a response, and the first and best responders are their parents.

It only takes a new mother a very few hours or days to get to know what a baby needs, since most of the cries can be soothed by close warm contact with her. It is often stated that African babies never cry. They certainly do it far less than European and American babies. We in the West have somehow lost the wish to have our babies close to us, or have them with us all the time. There are many social factors causing this, but from a purely selfish point of view we would be wiser to keep our babies close to our bodies for their first few weeks, and avoid the strain of crying anxieties. The quality of reassurance that a baby gets from being held or carried by its mother, moving with her, warmed by her, listening to her heart beat, her breathing rhythm, her voice, learning all the time, is hard to measure. The baby learns to sleep when it needs to sleep, no matter what is going on around it, and probably sleeps far more than when alone in a cot, and this is a wonderful advantage for the future.

Since Western women are unused to carrying weights around with them during their daily activities, they will find ways of modifying the routine to suit their particular baby and themselves. Fathers are now carrying their babies close to them when they can, and this gives their baby two people by whom it is refreshed and reassured. The involvement of the father with the baby at this early age is one of the greatest benefits of modern parental care.

As the baby grows a little older, its crying will indicate new needs. It learns to watch and look at things when awake, and may be bored when it wakes after sleeping in a cot or pram. It may wake up feeling too hot, or too cold, or wanting to change position and being unable to do so without help. It may want movement to help it to get back to sleep again — it has been moved continually in the womb, and certainly may miss the rocking motion. Jiggling up and down is not the movement it needs. Think of the way your body sways as you walk, or swings as you turn to take things or put them down in your office or kitchen. Jolting a baby up and down only attempts to distract him for a little while from whatever is worrying him, and if it fails to soothe him you are once again feeling a failure at being unable to stop the crying.

Most mothers find that feeding is a good way to soothe their newborn babies. This again is a deeply programmed response to a baby's crying, since newborn babies need feeding very often through the 24 hours. A study has been done on the length of time that newborn mammals feed their young and its relationship with the fat and protein content of the mother's milk, finding that the animal with the richest milk is a rabbit. A rabbit mother only suckles her young for an average of two minutes in 24 hours. Next is the seal, which suckles about four minutes a day and then a steady progression of other mammals; on this scale human beings come out as continuous feeders! So it is no surprise that so many new mothers wail that for the first week or two they seem to be feeding the baby all the time. The trouble is that we do not organize our lives to make this time of adjustment easy to fit in with everything else, nor do we recognize how important it is, nor how much time and worry it saves us later on if the settling in is given priority for a month or two after birth, for everyone concerned.

It is when a baby cries and cries and seems not to be able to be comforted that acute anxiety sets in. Most mothers then immediately blame themselves for lack of skill. It is more effective if they stop blaming and look for reasons.

In the first few hours, or even the first week or two, it may be that the baby is feeling the effects of drugs it has received through the placenta during the labour of its birth. It is a help to think how you felt yourself the day after the birth, or when you have a headache and can't take aspirin or something else to relieve the pain. The baby may well have a headache after its birth, especially if it has been delivered with the help of forceps. Or it may be quite bewildered by its sensations and only be able to sleep through exhaustion.

It is very frustrating and upsetting for a mother to have the baby reach the stage where even suckling at her breast is no comfort. She may feel rejected at a very basic level, and once again a failure as a mother. Usually nothing could be less true, and if she were less tired and anxious she would know it. Something else is the cause of crying, and sometimes a change of arms and voice will work the miracle.

Fathers are wonderful at this point. I remember walking the floor in the night with one of my babies who had got beyond the point of sleep, and not being able to think what else to do, or how I could stand it any longer, In tears, very tired, almost desperate, it seemed the ultimate insult that my husband could be sweetly sleeping through the racket when I didn't know what on earth to do. The baby of course sensed my rising panic, felt insecure, and cried the more. At last I put her down on the pillow beside him so that she was bawling right in his ear, and stormed at him that he must take her or I might throw her out of the window. He rose, with stately dignity, scooped her up and walked downstairs with her, as I flopped into bed weeping, and the little darling went straight to sleep in his arms, in about five minutes! It took me some time to console myself that she had been so worn out with crying that we were both as distressed as each other, and the transfer to a warm, calm, deep-voiced person was all she needed to bring her relief in sleep at last. Fathers can be so marvellous.

Hearing a baby crying for a long time is very distressing for the mother and the father, let alone neighbours and friends. Provided you are sure that your baby is not hungry, has a clean nappy, and is warm, then crying for a short while will do no harm. But the anxiety this raises in you is difficult to keep under control. Many parents use a dummy to help their babies get to sleep comfortably. Others have very strongly held views against the use of dummies. My own view is that, wisely used, a dummy can be a great help.

It is much much later that crying can be attributed to temper, or be in any way deliberate. If a good relationship has been established in the first few difficult weeks, then the mother will quickly detect the new sort of crying, and that is a whole new ball-game.

There is also the cry that tells of pain and illness, and it is reassuring to know that mothers very swiftly can recognize this from other cries. If a baby is in pain internally, it will double its knees up to the stomach and twist its arms and body, and resist soothing. If a baby has a fever at the onset of infection it may be hot and wet with sweat, listless, and cry miserably or weakly. If you suspect that your baby is ill, or if you are worried but not quite sure why, go to your doctor or health visitor quickly. They will never mind being asked, and would far rather reassure you that it is a false alarm than deal with acute illness which could have been avoided.

Interviews with mothers

When I talked to mothers of young children about how they coped when their babies cried a lot and could not sleep, I got no quick, fail-safe remedies. Everyone knew the difficulty, and was aware that each baby varied in the amount of time he cried and in the way in which he could be soothed. Everyone had been imaginative and resourceful in trying this and that until the baby had settled into some sort of routine. This happened for all of them at between two and three months, when the baby was beginning to be more interested in the outside world, taking notice, looking around and moving its head and limbs with more definite purpose.

Maureen 'If my baby cried a lot during the day, and I knew he wasn't hungry but just overtired, I simply went out for a walk, with him in the sling. When he got too heavy for that, I'd take him in the pram, and once or twice Paddy resorted to driving him around in the car to let him get to sleep. It always worked; the movement and the fresh air, and perhaps the steady noise of the car engine, or the wind in the trees or passing cars soothed him better than anything else.

'I didn't go along with demand feeding. It seemed to end up with the baby being put back to suck when he didn't really need more food — and I had no more to give him — so we both got upset. I got both my babies into a routine as soon as possible. They were much happier that way, and so was I. When I knew they had had a good breastfeed, I thought they needed sleep more than sucking for comfort, and taking them out walking was my way to help them. Both of them learned to suck their thumbs after a month or two.'

Ilsa 'I think the jazzy colours and complicated cots that so many babies have to try to sleep in don't help at all. In my country, Denmark, we use simple cots which can be rocked by a foot pedal. They are lined with soft colours and natural fabrics, soft cotton or silk. It's very restful for a mother to sit peacefully and rock her baby to sleep — she can rest or knit or read at the same time. We shade our babies in their cots. We think that strong light is a strain for them and keeps them awake, and we use the colours of the sky for shading — blue and gentle sunset colours. I found that humming helped to soothe a baby if it cried a lot, just a quiet continuous hum on a low single note. Sometimes, too, I would give the baby a warm bath — not hot, just warm — with either calendula or lavender oil in it. Both of those oils are very sleep-inducing and calming.'

Helen 'If my baby couldn't sleep during the day I used to take her out for a walk, whatever the weather. The change and hearing different noises from those inside the house used to distract her, and the movement calmed her. It did me good too, and stopped me feeling trapped indoors with a baby I couldn't soothe. Only once did I feel absolutely desperate and didn't know what to do, and then I phoned a friend who had offered to help if the need arose. She came straight round and told me to go and have a long hot soak in a bath and relax, while she carried my baby and rocked her to sleep. That was all the baby wanted, a change of arms, and after that I didn't ever panic again.

'At night Tim and I used to share the getting up if it was necessary. Once the baby could be distracted by new sights and sounds it really wasn't a problem any more.'

Ann 'If my baby cried a lot I'd always check everything first to see whether I'd tied up his bootees too tight, or stuck his nappy to his skin, or whatever. After that, if he was fed and had burped, and I'd done everything I could, I didn't try to feed him any more. I couldn't ever shut him in a room and go away out of hearing — I think that could be very dangerous. Suppose he was sick and choked? I'd stay with him and switch off — read or do something to occupy myself, and lift him every five or ten minutes and get up the wind which he'd swallowed because of the crying. He very soon learned to cry for only a very little time and then drop off to sleep.'

Feeding

It really is extraordinary that it is necessary to write books about breastfeeding. It is such a spontaneous activity after a baby is born, and most women and babies would be 'doing what comes naturally' but for the overlay of inherited attitudes.

For lots of reasons breastfeeding went out of fashion after the Second World War, and by 1960 in Britain only one in ten babies were breastfed. The technology for treating milk and storing it as powder for instant reconstitution with water had been perfected, along with all other food processing, and prepared cows' milk was believed to be a totally acceptable substitute for human milk and quite safe for babies. It has taken over twenty years for doubts to creep in about this. The increase in allergic reactions in children to cows' milk and dairy products as a result of putting babies on to cows' milk immediately after birth is now well recognized.

Even more important is the value of colostrum — the first secretion from the mother's breasts after birth and before the true milk comes in — to the baby for health and survival. Colostrum is a true Wonder Substance. It starts the digestive processes in the baby's gut, which has never been used, since during pregnancy the baby has been fed in the uterus through its bloodstream, not its mouth. It is also rich in antibodies from the mother which it confers on the baby, so that if the mother has had measles and chicken pox and other ailments, she gives some protection to her baby through the colostrum. These common diseases of childhood can be killers for babies when they are newly born, so being able to give the baby such effective protection is a great relief.

The revival of breastfeeding and the gradual growth of recognition of the importance of human breastmilk to the newborn baby started in the United States at the same time as women in Britain were beginning to get worried about its decline. Organizations such as the National Childbirth Trust and the La Lèche League from America helped mothers who wanted to breastfeed their babies and supported them through the current anti-breastfeeding attitudes. Gradually leaflets and books were written giving information and helpful advice. But it was not until there was an outbreak of gastroenteritis in a Midlands maternity hospital in the early 1970s, during which twenty-eight out of thirty babies died, and the two survivors were the only two who were breastfed, that the medical establishment as a whole began actively to encourage mothers to breastfeed again.

As usual when a revival takes place, some people become fanatical about their wish to bring about change, and this can have the effect of antagonizing other undecided people. The case for breastfeeding a newborn baby is almost unassailable except in very few cases and for exceptional reasons. But the continuation of breastfeeding over months is very much an individual matter for each mother to decide for herself in her own situation.

It helps a good deal if breastfeeding has been well established while you are in hospital. Then there are no worries when you come back home about sterilizing bottles or teats, composition of the milk, or why the baby may not take the 'proper amount' at every feed. Babies, like adults, don't want exactly the same amount of food at every meal. Sometimes they have slept for a long stretch, and wake up feeling starving hungry; at other times they may have stayed awake or cat-napped, and want just a light snack. Once established, breastfeeding is so easy; the milk is perfect for the baby, right heat, right mixture, always available, comes on supply and demand.

The catch phrase is 'once established', because there seems to be a great deal of anxiety around about getting the baby feeding very soon after it has been born, and anxiety makes for tension which doesn't help in the least. Newborn babies often want to suckle at their mother's breast almost at once after they are born, especially if the mother has had few drugs during labour and the baby is alert. Indeed, the sucking reflex is at its strongest in the first 24 hours after birth.

There is an art and a skill in getting the baby and the mother together, with the baby properly latched on to the nipple so that she or he can use the magnificent sucking action to the best advantage. When that happens it feels just right for the mother too. Haste and hurry are no help at all to a mother learning how to get her first baby sucking well at her nipple. Given peace and time, and no feeling of anxious rush, almost every mother will work it out with her baby, so long as she does not feel that she *must*, right there and then, at the first attempt.

It is reassuring to remember that the baby will not suffer starvation if he fails to feed easily for quite a long time. Anyone who remembers the Mexican earthquake, when babies were rescued from the rubble up to nineteen days after the disaster, having been without any food all that time, and survived, will not be likely to worry unduly if a newborn baby in a warm hospital takes some hours to get familiar with how to get the nipple well into its mouth. If the mother is keen to give milk, and the baby is keen to get it, they will find the way, and the skill is quickly learned.

The baby's expressions and efforts are endearing, and can be very funny. With patience and a good deal of humour the new mother can get used to the strange new sensations, and is usually very surprised when she first feels a proper sucking action from the baby. It's so strong, not painful, but unusual.

If, however, the hospital has rules about the time of the first feed, and if the midwife is under pressure to make sure the baby is fed, tension can swiftly build up. Then, if the first attempt is not successful, the mother tends to feel tearful and a failure. If the baby is then given even a small amount of milk from a bottle, the whole thing becomes much harder. The baby will not be so hungry next time he tries to feed from his mother, may fall asleep in the middle of the feed, and the mother's frustration mounts; it all gets difficult, and sometimes a nightmare, which ends with the mother being put off this way of feeding altogether.

For women to breastfeed their babies happily and without anxiety I think two things are necessary. The first is that they deserve to have available all the information about the advantages and disadvantages for the baby and for themselves, so that they can make an informed choice about breastfeeding, and they need support and encouragement in the first days when the breastfeeding is being established. The second is that they know that they are free to give up breastfeeding whenever they decide the right time has come for themselves and their baby, in whatever situations are operating for them.

Many women love breastfeeding their babies and find great joy and comfort in the closeness and warmth between them. Others find the whole business of breastfeeding unattractive and messy, and dislike milk leaking from their breasts and the feeling of being like a cow on tap at all times. These women will breastfeed out of sheer love for the good of their baby, and may decide to stop very soon after the first few important days. Between the two extremes are the widest variety of women's feelings and practices.

My own approach to breastfeeding is to plead for the baby to get colostrum as a priority, on grounds of health and welfare for the future. After that, give the breastfeeding a whirl — hospitals and domiciliary midwives are not going to 'dry you up' these days because the hormone treatment necessary to do this has been proved to be dangerous. So there's the milk, and there's the baby, try putting them together and see what it's like. If you enjoy it, great; if you don't, then every day you've tried is a bonus for the baby and worth the effort. If you manage five days of full breastfeeding that's good; if you manage five weeks, that's even better; if you manage five months that's superb.

If you find that you simply abhor the breastfeeding, or if you decide that because of your life and its commitments breastfeeding for a long time is quite out of the question, then transfer to a good brand of cow's milk powder, and feel good about your decision.

If you want to carry on breastfeeding as long as possible, even though your work commitments make it hard to do so, or your home situation is very difficult, you can breastfeed flexibly by expressing milk for someone else to feed to the baby from a bottle in your absence. Some women do this quite successfully, and there are good breast-pumps available now which make expressing far easier than it used to be. But some babies simply will not suck from a bottle once they are used to sucking from a breast. Manufactured rubber teats used to be completely unlike human teats which added to the problem, but there are now some bottles and teats on the market which have copied the human-shaped nipple, and it is worth hunting for these if you want to bottle-feed your baby at any time. Expressed breastmilk can also be frozen for later use.

Special Cases

Babies born with variations from the normal such as cleft palate, or weak sucking reflex after a difficult birth, or some genetic disorders, may be unable to feed from the breast, and for them bottle-feeding is life-saving, Specially modified teats can be made, to make sucking easy and effective.

Another special case is that of premature babies, who may not be mature enough to have developed a strong sucking reflex. They may have to be tube-fed until they have caught up in age with the stage of full-term birth. Or they may be able to take milk in very small amounts with a specially modified bottle, and these can be given their mother's milk, if she expresses it daily and supplies it to the hospital. For these babies breastmilk is of very great importance, and many Special Care Baby Units have 'milk banks' which freeze breastmilk brought in by mothers and use it when needed. Mothers who are successfully breastfeeding their babies and have more than enough milk can express the surplus and supply it to these Units to help premature babies survive, and it is a wonderful thing to do.

If you are one of the mothers who need to travel in to the hospital each day to see your baby in a SCBU, help with transport is very valuable. If hospitals cannot provide such help, friends and families often do, and also charities such as the National Childbirth Trust when the mother has been a member of one of their classes.

If you needed the help of forceps, or a Caesarean section for the birth of your baby, it is easy to expect that breastfeeding will be more difficult, or impossible to get going. Certainly support and help is very important, because the positioning of the baby makes such a difference when sitting up is difficult because of stitches. Breastmilk is known to be the best for babies overcoming stress of any sort, especially if they are premature, and the closeness and warmth between the baby and the mother helps healing in body and mind, Most of all the desire to breastfeed often makes the difference between ease and difficulty. I talked to one mother who seemed to have everything stacked against her, but found the help she needed close at home.

Interview with Juliet, who breastfed her baby after a Caesarean section

Juliet is a New Zealander living in Europe, and had her first baby in a foreign culture. Two weeks before her due date she was advised to have a Caesarean section because of complications in the position of the baby. She agreed. After the birth the baby had breathing difficulties and was whisked away immediately to a SCBU. She was encouraged to produce milk for the baby, and given a breast pump which her husband helped her to use so that he could take the milk to the SCBU, which was in a different building. After four days the baby was re-united with his mother, and they spent two more days there before returning home.

Juliet 'I had no statutory help at all from the equivalent of Health Visitors except for one visit when my baby was two months old — and that only because he had been in a SCBU after being born. But Lucas took to the breast with no problems, and my husband was at ease with the whole business and very much in favour of breastfeeding, so he gave me strong support. I'd had nothing to do with babies before, but Kevin is the oldest in a big family and he taught me everything — how to hold Lucas and bath him and soothe him. He really 'mothered' me and that was *such* a help.

'But my baby hadn't regained his birth weight when I went to see the paediatrician three weeks later, and I was advised to give him supplementary bottles. I did this for a month — always the breast first, and then topped him up from the bottle. There was nobody nearby to advise me, but I telephoned La Lèche League who had a group there. They gave me strong encouragement to continue, and I got him back on to full breastfeeding. Then we went on holiday back to New Zealand and he put on 2 kilos in a month! So I was a successful breastfeeder. I didn't enjoy having to give it up when I went back to work when Lucas was four months old — I'd have liked to continue until he was six months. You only get ten months' maternity leave here, but the firm I work for was very helpful and let me have extra leave.

'I think all new mothers who want to breastfeed need special help and support at the very beginning. I couldn't have done it without my husband, especially as there is no special enthusiasm for breastfeeding as a priority here, and *very* little help at home. It was possible for us as Kevin is self-employed and works from home, and he could juggle time in the early days when we came home from hospital, I found getting back to normal much more difficult than I'd expected — there was absolutely no preparation beforehand for the pain, for one thing, or the healing time after a major operation, which a Caesar is.'

There are many excellent books available to give detailed advice and help on the techniques of breastfeeding and its importance. If you are in difficulty or doubt, a phone call to the National Childbirth Trust or La Lèche League (see page 191) will put you in touch with a breastfeeding counsellor at any time of the day or night. She will listen and help over the phone, or visit quickly if she can. It is in the first four weeks that help and reassurance is usually needed, and it's a comfort to know that such people are around.

How long to breastfeed?

The problem of how long to breastfeed worries many new mothers. 'When should I stop feeding?' is a frequent question even before the baby is born. The answer really is to wait and see how it goes. Sometimes the baby makes the decision for you. Breastfeeding may be well established and everyone is happy, and then suddenly the baby refuses the breast, and doesn't want to feed, and you wonder what on earth is wrong, and what to do now. This can be temporary, because you have eaten something which the baby detects and doesn't like, or because the first stirrings of teeth growing up through the baby's gums make sucking painful, or one of many other reasons. But it can also be permanent, and the baby decides that sucking milk from a breast is just too much hard work, and she or he would prefer to get the drink much quicker from a cup or a bottle.

Unless there are special reasons for breastfeeding a baby for a very long time, I am not at all sure that long-continued breastfeeding *is* the best thing for the child. It may be the situation that the *mother* needs and wants, and that may be a good reason for continuing past a year. My own feeling is that it is probably wisest to wean the baby on to a cup for drinking milk or on to a bottle, before the child is aware that he or she is being denied the breast when the time for weaning comes. For most children this is usually sometime between nine months old and one year. It's much harder for a child over a year old to be told that Mum no longer wishes to allow her or him to suckle at her breast, and at that age the reasons for the mother's decision may be quite strange and incomprehensible. It just seems like rejection.

It helps breastfeeding to go well if you can avoid feeling anxious about things while you are feeding. Breastfeeding is so blessedly flexible, and the happiest situation is when a mother is relaxed and contented to give time and interest to the baby with her milk. The biggest enemy once again is tiredness because it's so easy to blame the breastfeeding for the tiredness. In fact, looking after a young baby is tiring, not breastfeeding by itself. So if you are tired it's difficult to decide which of the many factors in your life to blame, and often breastfeeding is the easiest.

Nevertheless if you do decide to change from breast to bottle-feeding, the balance of minerals and salt in cows' milk is different from human milk. Breastmilk is sweeter and has less salt in it than cows' milk, so a baby who changes to a saltier drink will be more thirsty. The trap when this happens is that mothers may think the baby needs more milk when he or she is thirsty, and this overloads the baby's stomach with extra food, and doesn't solve the thirstiness. What a bottle-fed baby may well need if dissatisfied are more drinks of water.

Personal experiences

When I spoke to different mothers about it, I received various responses about the advantages and disadvantages of breastfeeding:

> **Lucy** 'With my first baby, Madeleine, I was massively confident, and didn't expect problems. Because I was in a single room, out of the limelight, and no one gave me any advice, I found it easy to muddle along and learn. I found it easy once I'd learnt to get as much of me into her mouth as possible, so that she wasn't chomping on my nipple, which

makes you sore. Madeleine was a good sucker, which helped. I found the let-down reflex quite painful to begin with, but I felt it was a good, positive pain. From then on it was prime and easy — but it did make you tired.

'My second baby (William) was quite different. Again I was very confident and knew I could do it. But William didn't want to feed much in the first day or two, and I worried because I felt he should have been feeding every four hours. It was difficult to relax. Getting him latched on was *very* frustrating, because he kept his tongue on the roof of his mouth, so that the nipple couldn't get in for him to suck. If I hadn't had the previous experience and calm knowledge, I would have found it very difficult, especially when my breasts were full and tender. I found that *understanding* why things were happening made it easier to cope with. I found that angles were quite important — holding him across my body, as I had done with Maddy, made it more difficult to help him keep his tongue down, and you seem to need three hands for that anyway! But I found it all painful — it's not easy to establish even when done before. There were times when I only carried on because it was best for the baby. My doctor told me that mothers so often give up after six or seven weeks, and that's often just when you get it properly established. I think it's important to give yourself time, give 'getting established' a loose lead — with Maddy I 'established' early, with William it was not until much later at five to six weeks.'

Janet 'I decided to breastfeed because it was the best thing for my baby, but I missed the breastfeeding class in my antenatal course, and I didn't know how to cope when difficulties began. To start with it wasn't painful or difficult. But then I got tense and my baby was upset and chewed a lot, which made me sore. I was sore anyway from stitches, so the whole lot felt awful, and I nearly gave up.

'I received help from two midwives in the hospital, who showed me different positions, so that I could relax, and the pain went. The stitches, piles, and being very tired after the birth made sitting up painful, and they showed me how to feed lying on my side. Now I'm back on my feet, but I still have various problems, with my breasts going white towards the end of a feed. I talked to a breastfeeding counsellor and she told me how to help that, using massage at the end of a feed, and warm flannels, and I can cope. I've read about other women having this reaction, so I'm not on my own. My family and friends are very supportive.

'I'm returning to part-time work soon, so I will introduce a bottle; he's happy with this every now and then at the moment, but I'll do it more regularly nearer the time. I hope to bottle-feed while I'm at work, and breastfeed when I'm at home.'

Kate 'I intended to breastfeed, but wasn't sure I would be able to. I've not got big breasts, and I didn't believe I'd have enough milk. I'm very pleased that I can! My son sucked well, and knew how to latch on after a little nuzzling around at first. It hurt a bit, and I wasn't given *nearly* enough information about how to establish breastfeeding and make sure the baby really had the nipple well back in his mouth. The result was that my nipples got very sore, and bled, and friends advised me to use a nipple shield. That helped a lot for a couple of days and made me able to carry on, but then my midwife told me that I must go back to feeding without the shield, and get the baby sucking properly — and now it is so easy.

'It's a funny feeling when you are sore, and the moment comes to put the baby on to his feed. As his head comes nearer you draw back, because you know the first suck is going to hurt — it's like a slow movement in a dance! I needn't have had all that, if I'd been given better help at the very first about how to get him feeding easily. The most useful instruction for feeding was that even if you *are* sore, you must move towards the baby as you put him to your breast, even if all your instincts are to pull away! It makes all the difference.'

Charlotte 'I'm very happy breastfeeding, and it's going fine. I've always thought a baby was meant to feed that way — I never thought anything else. My mum is a health visitor and very pro-breastfeeding; and my baby helped — he knew what to do! I read a lot, and asked other mothers who were breastfeeding for tips. My mum was very helpful, and the midwives in hospital gave positive help when asked to adjust my positioning.

'Establishing it was much easier than I thought. The midwives in hospital waited to be asked for help, which was alright for me, but not so good for those mothers who hadn't read or found out about how to start. One midwife told me to watch my baby's ear and jaw action, listen to the swallowing noise and look for slow, rhythmic feeding. That was very helpful. I had cracked nipples, probably due to wrong positioning at the start, but I knew they wouldn't last long, and I coped by visualising a river and water, to help me relax and the milk flow quickly, and that was very good. I also used 'Camilosan' cream — my baby liked the taste, and it's healing.'

Breastfeeding advantages

CONVENIENCE

No need to make up the right mix of milk, or get it to the right heat before giving it to the baby. The milk you make is always just as it should be for the baby, and is on tap whenever the baby is hungry. No need to have a frustrated, screaming, hungry baby to deal with.

CHEAPNESS

Milk you make yourself automatically costs nothing. Formula bought at a chemist or grocer costs a lot.

SAFETY

Human milk is the right composition for human babies. Cows' milk contains unwanted chemicals from agricultural pesticides and growth hormones, which increasingly set up allergic reactions in babies. Care must also be exercised over the sterilization of bottles and teats, which are sources of disease if not properly cleaned.

HEALTH

Human milk has very little residue after digestion by the baby. The composition is so balanced that the baby absorbs almost all of it. Breastfed babies can go for several days without passing a motion, quite safely, or they can also have a dirty nappy every day, or at every feed; each is quite normal, so worries about digestion are removed. Breastfed babies are lively and compact, because the balance of minerals is correct for human babies. Cows' milk, on the other hand, has a different balance of minerals (correct for calves), so that the residue is greater and bottle-fed babies should always do a motion every day. They are more likely to suffer from constipation. Bottle-fed babies may suffer from overweight; breastfed babies do not.

Another advantage is that in order to breastfeed, mothers need to feed themselves well, a factor that can easily be overlooked at this time but which is vital to the woman's physical and emotional wellbeing.

EMOTIONAL BENEFITS

Feeding a baby yourself is for many women a very special delight. The feeling of warmth and closeness with the baby and the knowledge that you are giving it the best can be deeply rewarding. Other benefits are that when feeding a baby you *must* sit down and relax, which ensures that new mothers get seven or eight opportunities for relaxation every day.

Breastfeeding disadvantages

EARLY DIFFICULTIES

Establishing breastfeeding can be quite a struggle. When the milk first comes into your breasts, about three days after the baby's birth, you may have a day or two of overfull breasts, which feel hot and heavy, and very strange indeed the first time it happens. Because your breasts are so full the baby finds it difficult to suck the nipple, and since you need the baby to suck strongly and relieve the fullness of the breasts, frustration mounts. For the first few weeks, also, your breasts produce more milk than the baby can drink at each feed, and may leak frequently. Many women find this damp milky state unattractive and off-putting. It's a state which passes quickly, but seems to go on for ever.

RESPONSIBILITY

The awareness of the baby's total dependence on you for its very food and living weighs heavily on mothers. Women say they feel they simply *can't* be ill, or have an off day, because the baby will suffer and be hungry, and then of course the mother suffers too. Women are also frightened of having any sort of accident, because the separation from the baby would be so difficult for both of them. The impossibility of having a day off is also very hard for some women. They feel trapped by the baby's needs, as though on a treadmill, a willing, or not so willing, slave to their tiny child. This frustration can be greatly eased by knowing that you can mix breast and bottle feeding if you wish to. It's a bit of a fuss, but it can be done, and just knowing that it can be done is enough to make most mothers who feel trapped give a gasp of relief.

SOCIETY'S ATTITUDES

There is absolutely no doubt that mothers are not welcomed in most public places if they wish to feed their babies at the breast. The difficulties placed in a mother's ways are enormous. Very few shops, stations, bus stations or offices provide rooms where a mother can feed her baby in peace and comfort.

Both the National Childbirth Trust and La Lèche League campaign for more facilities to be made available for mothers who are breastfeeding their babies, and attitudes towards breastfeeding on trains, buses and aeroplanes are slowly changing for the better.

Feeding a baby can be done very discreetly — often people nearby are not even aware that a women has the baby at her breast. But if you do get an adverse reaction, it can be very distressing.

Sometimes you get a surprise. A young mother I know was feeding her baby in her own car in a public car park during a shopping trip, and was approached by an elderly woman. Expecting a criticism or a complaint, this mother was surprised and delighted when the woman said, 'How lovely to see someone breastfeeding a baby again! It used to be the normal thing when I was young and not nearly enough people do it now. Congratulations — you're doing the best for your baby.'

Tiredness

Tiredness is your biggest enemy as a new mother. Over and over again women say that they had no idea that a baby could take up so much time, or cause so much work. Being in hospital for the birth cushions the impact to some extent, but it means the parents and their child have a double start to go through. You come home, often tired already, because hospitals are never restful places, expecting to have a good sleep and recover your strength after the birth, in your own time. But you immediately find that the baby has quite other ideas. New babies need feeding every two or three hours at least for the first month and if you are used to having six or seven hours uninterrupted sleep each night this change alone will be a great shock.

With foreknowledge and care, much can be done to relieve tiredness, and avoid the sense of being overwhelmed by not just the last straw, but the whole strawstack. Fathers can, and do, help a very great deal — most of all by not expecting a beautifully tidy clean house, or a poised and relaxed companion every evening when they return from work. They, too, will find a new baby tiring; they will be needed to help more with domestic chores, and with entertaining the baby as it grows in alert understanding and interest.

The thing to keep in mind every moment of each day is that this extra-busy time does not last. The chaotic feeling of inability to cope *seems* to be everlasting while you're in it, but in reality it is only for a few weeks. Looking back afterwards parents say it wasn't really so bad, it just seemed it because no one could say when it would get easier. And they found it muddling and strange to be swayed so totally by so small a creature.

Mothers with only one child can easily catch up on their sleep by having a nap in the day whenever the baby does. The danger is that you may be tempted to use this quiet time to catch up on other things rather than catching up on your own sleep.

My most difficult time over tiredness came when I was having my fourth baby, very soon after the third. My two elder children were not yet at school (which was a blessing in a way, because walking to and fro to take and fetch them would have seemed impossible). My husband's job took him overseas a great deal, so he was often away. And our third child, who had been an angelic sleeper for his first ten months, became quite unable to sleep when he started to teethe, and for many weeks never slept for longer than twenty minutes at a time. I did get extremely tired, and what saved me was arranging for a kind elderly woman to take the three children for a walk each afternoon so that I could fall into bed and sleep without having an ear cocked all the time for my little son.

Since sleep is at a premium, and most women and men find it easier to sleep when the baby is asleep, or certainly not crying, then things which induce comfort and sleep for the baby are very important.

It is increasingly recognized that newborn babies dislike isolation, and feel lonely and unsure if left in loneliness and silence. Yet we as a society try to separate babies from their parents as soon as we can. This is counter-productive, since the more we push the baby away the more insecure it will feel and the more clinging it will become. Whereas if we make certain that the baby feels safe and secure in these very early days, it will branch out into life and develop independence much more quickly than it otherwise would. So you will find that keeping the baby physically close to you when it comes home from the hospital — and indeed in the hospital before it comes home — helps the baby to sleep and settle better.

Using a baby carrier, while the baby is small and light in weight, is marvellous, because the baby is rocked and soothed by your movements, and can hear the familiar parental heartbeat as its head lies against your chest or back.

Another investment in contented sleeping for the baby, and hence for mother and father too, is a specially cured and prepared lambskin for the baby to sleep on. Some years ago a researcher* carried out a comparative survey of four different ways of helping to reduce crying in young babies. One group of babies was put in ordinary cots; the second in Navajo baby cradles; the third in swaddling bands, as the Victorians used to do; and the fourth on lambskins in their cots. All three of the variations had good results in cutting down crying time and helping the babies to sleep better than the ones in conventional cots. Clearly all three made the babies feel comfortable and safe. The researcher used one of the Navajo baby cradles for his own baby, and sometimes brought her into the office in it and hooked it up on the wall, as the Red Indians do with their babies in the tepee or on a tree. The baby gurgled away to the people moving about below her very happily when she was awake! Lots to look at and interest her, and a comfortable place to drop off to sleep when she wanted. But not every office will accommodate a baby in this way, so perhaps baby cradles are the least ideal for Western life.

The lambskins, on the other hand, are available and growing in popularity. They are fully washable and come up soft and comfortable time and time again. A mother expecting her third baby told me she had taken a lambskin into hospital with her when she had her second baby and got him sleeping on it from the very beginning, and she was convinced that that had helped more than anything to make him such a good sleeper. The only children who cannot use them are babies who may have an allergic reaction to wool of any sort. Since this is an inheritable allergy, parents will probably be aware of it

*Martin Richards, Department of Medical Psychology, Cambridge

before considering buying a lambskin for their baby to sleep on.

Since shortage of sleep is such a universal problem for mothers after their first — and more particularly after their second or third — baby is born, I asked some parents whether they had any ways of dealing with tiredness which might be helpful to other new parents. Their answers were very consistent, and came from the heart.

Anne 'It's part of learning to be a mum — which means understanding that you simply can't do everything. First, it's much better *not* to try to keep your home perfect. I'd say to any new mother, "Don't try to be Superwoman".'

'So often, when people ask you how you are and if you need help, you are too proud to admit you're floundering, and you say you can cope. If someone says, "Can I do something to help?" say "Yes" and be glad to accept it thankfully. You only have to think what it's like to be on the *giving* end — it's disappointing if your offer of help is refused. It makes one feel so good when someone accepts your help when you want to give it. So, if you're very tired, accept help and give someone else pleasure! Ask for help if you need it, too. It's lovely to be asked. There's always a time in the future when you can repay the help by helping someone else, and the more friendly help there is around, the better.'

Di 'The biggest thing is to talk to someone. If you're very tired and you keep it to yourself you get more tired — it's a sort of downward spiral into depression. If you believe you're not coping you feel a failure, and that's tiring in itself. Life can seem so repetitive and boring. 'It's not the baby, it's the life that the baby needs you to get into — housework, cooking, washing, cleaning, etc.'

'The problem is the attitude of outside people, and often of the man in your life. Being a housewife is not rated highly. Women nowadays think they're doing "a good job" when they're outside their home. When you're inside, looking after the baby, and you can't even keep the house tidy, your self-image goes way down. I found it helped to talk to other women who understood, and made you see that the homemaking *is* important, *very* important, no matter what the outside world says as it whirls by. This is not an endless stage — it's quite like the tough patches in labour — they pass!'

Nicole 'Oh yes, I know all about that! That feeling that you're walking in a fog. The only thing you want to do is lie down and surrender to sleep, and there's no hope, the baby is there and needs this or that.

'We've had our children very close together, and I've got three under three years old, I think the most important thing is to sit and do nothing! Don't try to keep the house up to standard — and don't feel guilty, ever. The children are the most important thing, and if you try to go out visiting, or to do anything extra, it's a lot of work and you get even more tired. And then the kids sense it and you *all* get even more tired — and I'm so short tempered. So watch TV, read a book, sew, or just sit. Let the baby, or babies, sleep with you or play round you. That way everything doesn't get on top of you, and the babies don't get jittery.'

Twins

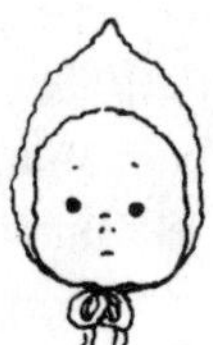
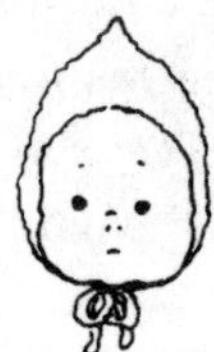

Parents are always surprised at the amount of time and energy they need for looking after a new baby. Obviously that surprise is doubled when twins are born — as are the time and energy needed to care for both babies. Consider the practicalities of feeding two newborn babies, each of whom may need milk every two hours at the start. Even when they have settled, more or less, into a four-hourly feeding routine, if both are hungry at the same time two pairs of hands are needed to avoid one or other twin becoming distressed and over-hungry because he or she must wait. If patient parents have managed to stagger the feed-times for the twins, so that they wake alternately every two hours, the days seem to be filled with nothing else but feeding, changing and soothing the babies.

At present, no statutory help is given by law to parents of twins. However, further multiple births — triplets, quadruplets etc. — have a right to daily help, and help with housing too. There is an association called TAMBA (Twins and Multiple Births Association) which supports families with twins, triplets or more, through local Twins Clubs and specialist support groups. It also promotes public and professional awareness of their needs. (See *Useful addresses* section on page 191.)

Breastfeeding twins can be done, and many mothers have managed to find ways to achieve this. In my experience it is mothers who have help from extended families, or who can pay for living-in or daily helpers, who breastfeed twins successfully. They either feed them together, one breast each (well supported with firm pillows, so that if one baby needs to bring up wind the other can continue to feed), or they feed them alternately. But without that extra pair of hands to help, it is very difficult for a mother to manage.

I asked a mother of twins to tell me how she had coped with the pressures of feeding and looking after her babies.

Margaret 'When the twins were born I was determined to breastfeed them, as I had my previous two single babies. I tried every way I could think of — lying back like a goddess earth mother with a twin on each breast, or feeding them alternately. It was definitely more difficult with twins, and took lots more time, but I think it would have been possible if they had been my *first* children. If twins come later in a family then you have to balance their needs with those of the older children. After a couple of weeks I had a bout of mastitis, and at three weeks I decided to swap to bottle-feeding.

'We had boy and girl twins, and from the very beginning they were so different, and always interesting. The older children were very different in their reaction to the twins. The elder was always happy to sit with one twin on her lap while the other was bathed or fed or had its nappy changed. But the younger, who was four, was definitely put off babies — I think it was because her nose was just at the height of the changing mat, so for some years babies meant a nasty smell! But the older ones are very proud of their twin siblings.

'The biggest lesson I learned was to accept help gracefully — and not to be proud and say I could manage on my own. I had a lovely older lady living nearby who offered to push the twins out in their pram one morning a week, or have them in her home if it was wet. That was a marvellous help, though I made a mistake in trying to catch up with cooking and cleaning on those mornings. I should have gone to bed and caught up with sleep instead. Until the twins were five months I coped pretty well, because we had room where we were living to put one twin, if he was restless, in a different room so that he would not wake up the other. My husband could also move into another room so that *he* would get some sleep.

'Our twins were crawling very early, and were trying to climb the stairs at six months old. They both walked at ten months. I found the most difficult time of day was between 5.30 pm and 7.00 pm, when they were tired and hungry and so were the two older children, not to mention us parents! So it was a long bedtime, with meals to be got ready and stories to be read — just too much to cram into the hours available. It was a good thing the twins played together so well. They were such fun too. It may have been busy, but it was a very happy and fulfilling time.'

Parents of twins all say how fascinating they are to bring up. In the first month they may seem to be endless work. Then, as they begin to smile and be interested in all that is going on around them, their own unique personalities start to show and they can be so very different from each other, especially if they are of different sexes. Even identical (fraternal) twins may develop at different speeds and show special abilities. Once they start to notice each other they entertain each other too, and this can be the greatest help for a busy mother or father. Babies love other babies and twins can be great companions.

Single Parents

Single mothers are in an especially difficult situation. Whether you are caring for your baby alone because of personal choice, death, or desertion, the lack of a loving companion with whom to share this big experience is very hard. The ups and the downs emphasise loneliness, and anxiety may make your relationship with the baby intense in several ways.

If you have chosen to embark on having the baby knowing you will be on your own during and after the birth, you will probably have thought about how you will cope, and tried to make some practical plans. Even so, reality when it comes may be very different from what you had expected. Hopefully, you have family and friends to turn to when in need. Whether society as a whole will give you strong support and help is another matter, influenced as it is by political theories and available resources.

If you are alone because of the death of the baby's father, you will be dealing with recent shock and deep grief and your emotions will be in turmoil. You may especially need people to talk with, and friends and counsellors who can understand your swings of feelings and give you confidence in your own ability to live through this difficult time. The baby's need of you and dependence on you may itself prove a lifeline in your difficulties. You cannot give up, because that would abandon your baby.

But if you are alone because your partner has decided that he does not like the prospect of fatherhood after all and has deserted you, then you may be in an even bigger boiling of emotions. Joy and love for the baby can be swamped by feelings of loss and rejection, anger, bewilderment, fear, loneliness and depression. Through all of this the baby can prove to be the one point of contact which does not fail you, the one person who instinctively loves and needs you without complications — your anchor in a rough sea.

Your anchor, but also your ball and chain. You may feel passionately protective and possessive about this tiny person to whom you have given birth, even to the point of being afraid to let her or him out of your sight or be handled by anyone else, for fear of losing your baby too. But also there will be times when you feel trapped, and horrified at the enormity of the years ahead, and yearn to be free again — the weight of sole responsibility for a child is so heavy. Then, being a woman, you add guilt to your burden. It seems as though you have let your child down in your mind by wishing he or she were not there!

Being left alone by the baby's father may rock your confidence severely. Especially if this baby was planned and agreed, in or out of marriage. The unfairness of the situation hits you squarely; *you* have carried this baby, grown her, given birth to her and because of this you are linked to the baby in a very special way. *He* has not had all this experience, and can swan off saying he finds the sudden realisation of responsibility too threatening and he's not ready for it. In a way, parenthood comes naturally to most women; it has to be worked at by many men especially if they have been brought up (by women) to expect to be of first importance themselves. The arrival of a new baby who is in the star spot can be a horrid shock to a new father. He may react against the whole business of time, money and energy poured out for the baby, and decide this is not his scene at all.

It is too easy for a man to behave in this way in an unstructured relationship, and at the time of writing this is happening too often for comfort. It happens even if the parents are married, but then the deserted wife does have legal rights — for which she may have to fight, on top of all her other troubles. But she *is* protected by law to some extent in terms of maintenance and money. Only if the baby's father has been cruel or perverted in some way does a woman feel some sense of relief at finding herself a single parent.

Teenage single parents

The prospect of being a single parent when you are very young, in your teens, is difficult and very frightening. However it came about that you are pregnant, you are suddenly faced with big decisions with long-term consequences, which must be made quickly. The most urgent is whether you want this baby to continue, or whether you want a termination of the pregnancy — which must be done before 24 weeks' gestation. Which is right for you? If you have the baby, how can you support him or her? Do you believe that abortion is never a good thing? What do your parents and your boyfriend think? Do they even know? Will you be able to continue your education, whatever stage you are at? Who will look after your baby while you get on with your education so that you can make a career?

These are such important questions to face alone. You may not so far have had to make decisions which will map out your future. So the first thing to do is to talk to someone older whom you can trust. Your parents are the nearest and should be your best help and support — and if you are under sixteen they are legally responsible for you, and must know about your pregnancy. However difficult, the sooner they know the better, even if they are shocked or angry, or very sad about it. If you cannot talk to them, for any reason, find someone else, a teacher or a counsellor; or go to a Brook Advisory Centre (see page 191). Although you don't know them, they are not going to be critical; they are unbiased and confidential and will help you break the news to the people who must know if they are to help you along the way you choose.

The worst thing you can do is to do nothing. You need wise and open-minded help to sort out the many things you must decide so quickly, because you probably still cannot believe you are going to have a baby.

Finding support

However a mother finds herself alone as a parent, and whatever age she is, she needs to have faith in herself and in her ability to care for and love her baby. If she has a religious faith that gives her a sense of her own value, that's a great help. But if this faith makes her feel guilty, then it adds to her anxieties and needs to be sorted out.

If she has only herself to rely on, her roots must be strengthened, wherever they lie. Family and friends have a duty to give her support and encouragement to find her feet, and embark on bringing up her child alone. Whatever mistakes or misjudgments have been made — about which she will be only too aware, and doesn't need them ramming home — or however often she has been warned of disaster ahead, the immediate concern is the baby's health and well-being. That is inextricably bound up with the mother. Recriminations are useless. Help with the washing and ironing, cooking and sleeping, clothes, food and money are what counts.

Single fathers are not so numerous as single mothers, which is a blessing because a father left alone with a new baby, through death or desertion, has even more to cope with than a mother. Added to the loss, sorrow, loneliness, anger, rejection and depression is often helplessness, fear and panic at the enormity of the task of immediate caring for the baby. Men are not biologically programmed to grow babies and instinctively take on the feeding and nurturing after birth. The sheer physical needs are bewildering. A man cannot breastfeed the baby and must learn fast the mechanics of bottle-feeding, washing, changing nappies (diapers), soothing, and rocking to sleep if he plans to take on the total care of his child. If that is impossible, and for most men it is, he must seek and find a substitute mother, and very quickly too. He too, needs the help and support of family, friends and society.

The duty towards single parents extends to society as a whole. Babies are the nation's future, and any country which fails to give strong and practical support to new parents does not deserve to have a healthy, happy and hard-working generation growing up for the future. Along with that, if women have found their menfolk fail them in time of need, we should look carefully at the way we bring up our sons! 'The hand that rocks the cradle rules the world' — and lays foundations.

Interviews with single parents

I talked with two single mothers, one of whom had received strong support from her family and the other had not. The responsibilities and fears for the future were the same, and their solutions — going back to work and using available nursery school help — developed along the same lines. But their experiences during the first months after the baby's birth were very different.

The first mother, Cyrilla, had been living with her partner for seven years before she found she was pregnant. She was a lonely girl, her father having died when she was two and her mother when she was seventeen, and her only sister lived a long way away. Because of the coming baby she and her partner decided to marry. He had a son by a previous relationship and was longing for a daughter. He was delighted with her but would do nothing to help, and seemed to have lost all interest in Cyrilla, now that she had produced what he wanted and was physically not so attractive.

> **Cyrilla** 'I found I got more and more depressed and lonely. I was jealous of my baby because he loved her and not me. There was no one to turn to, no one came to offer help, no parents, no one of my own near. And *I'd* already changed, because I was thinking about the baby's future, and I saw that

I'd have to do everything myself — he was not going to help at all.'

After some months she took her daughter and went to visit her sister, and then an aunt who lived even further away. During her absence her partner took up with someone else. They divorced and she accepts that, although her ex-husband loves to see his daughter and show her off, he is glad to bring her back after a day and she will bring up her child on her own.

She says:

'I would *never* recommend anyone to have a baby knowing they would be a single parent. It is *very* hard work, and a big responsibility. You need a lot of help, which you usually do not get, unless you have a family who loves you. My daughter is three-and-a-half now and she's lovely.'

The second single mother I interviewed was Lisa. She is working to support her daughter Amy, who is eighteen months old now. She never planned or expected to be bringing up a child on her own. She had always thought she would give up work and look after her child full time for several months or years when the time came. But she became pregnant while in a relationship which she knew would not survive the arrival of a child. In spite of that, and all the future difficulties, she decided against abortion.

Lisa 'My daughter was born prematurely, at thirty weeks. When I brought her home she was tiny. My parents were very supportive to me throughout, and the Special Care Baby Unit was excellent — it was they who recommended me to a very good nursery for babies. I had to go back to work as soon as possible, and luckily I had a good job. Amy was born in August, and I went back to work in January.

'The nursery takes babies from the age of one month until they are two years old. They get *very* good care there, daily from 8 am till 6 pm, on a weekly payment basis, and if you need extra hours because of overtime, they will keep them later at an hourly rate. She has been happy there, and has always had other babies to live and grow with, as she could have in an ordinary family.

'When she was sixteen months, I thought it would be better to have a daily nanny at my home, so that Amy could be there all the time. It would also cut my commuting time, and make my daily working life more flexible. I engaged a young nanny, and she's been looking after Amy for the last two months.

'However, there have been problems with the nanny. She is young and indulges my toddler in order to avoid the temper tantrums which will happen when she can't have what she wants. So *I'm* the person who says 'No' and I get all the tantrums and sad feelings!

'Another problem is the cost. The day nanny is paid as much as the nursery (including extra hours for the overtime I work), and I have to pay tax on top. There are also some hidden costs — I've just got the first telephone bill since she came, and it's *huge*!

'When Amy is in the nursery school, I know where she is and I can always reach her. But if I phone home and there is no answer, I don't know where the nanny is, or where she has taken Amy, or why, so my anxiety level is much higher. And then there is the question of influence; it's difficult to know what sort of attitudes and interests the nanny is giving to Amy. Perhaps a lot of television - which I do not want. At the nursery there is structured and interesting play, and proper rest times, and other babies and toddlers to react to.

'I think my particular nanny situation would have been better if the person I'd chosen had been older and more experienced. If I ever engage another, I'll lay a much better basis of ground rules and make them clear from the start. But instead I've decided to return Amy to the nursery, where she was always happy.

'I can't see very far ahead — no one really can. But I am *very* lucky to be living near to this good nursery, and once Amy reaches two there is another nursery school nearby which takes children on to five years old, when they start proper school. This new school has a system of keeping the children on during school holidays for the first year or two.'

Relieving stress

In its worst cases, stress can lead to abusive behaviour. The abuse of babies and small children is a distressing subject. In recent years so much of it has come to light in the media that no one can ignore the realisation of widespread physical, sexual and mental abuse by some parents.

Discovering how cruelly some babies and toddlers are treated undermines the fragile confidence of all new parents. Especially if you are very tired or frustrated with a fretful baby, you may begin to fear that you too could lose control and harm your child — and which parent could honestly say they had *never* reached that point? Or you may start to suspect your own motives in keeping the baby in bed with you, stroking or cuddling him, or giving a soothing massage. That would be such a pity, because babies need close contact with the warmth and security of their parents, and suffer in other ways if they are pushed away by their parents.

In the first year, the physical abuse of a baby is the most common danger. This comes mainly from tiredness and stress in the new parents, especially from the mother who spends so many hours alone with her baby. Physical abuse can be understood — though not condoned — and helped (see the earlier chapter on Tiredness).

Only mentally sick individuals could take *pleasure* in the distress or pain of their baby, and if that is the case the baby needs rescue.

Weariness and depression, lack of money for help, poor housing, overcrowding, and criticism at the wrong time are powerful reasons for loss of control at difficult moments. But if control snaps, the baby should *never* be hit or shaken; it may be permanently damaged, which becomes a lifelong sorrow. Babies are vulnerable. Their muscles, bones and ligaments are soft and easily hurt by the strength and force of adults in anger or temper. Also, the strain on the parents is *very* much worse because guilt is added.

Sexual abuse of babies and toddlers, on the other hand, can *never* be excused. It is an intolerable exploitation of the weak and vulnerable by the very people who should be the child's protectors. Babies and children *must* trust their parents— they can do no other; these are the adults who have given them life, and on whom they are dependant for life to go on. If those adults use them for their own gratification, as objects who cannot refuse to take part, the physical pain and mental fear does untold harm. The child may never be able to grow into a full and happy experience of sexuality. Parents who tell their children that sexual actions, for which the child is nowhere near ready, are a sign of *loving* are abusing them mentally as well as physically. It is not loving to force your own will on someone who cannot oppose you.

One of the saddest results of such abuse is the fear that parents have, if they have themselves been abused as children. They may fear that any feelings of physical delight they have when they hold their own baby, or encircle their toddler with protective arms if he or she is frightened or hurt, is the beginning of 'wrong' feelings towards their child. For the great majority of parents it is impossible to imagine how anyone could exploit innocence in that way, and they are horrified at the thought that their delight and pride in their babies could degenerate into abuse, for their own brief pleasure. Most parents now have had to face up to their own sexuality in a way that previous generations have failed — or never felt the need — to do. It may be an extra stress, but it is also an opportunity to improve relationships between children and parents for long-term good.

Never be afraid to seek help, if you feel you are getting to the end of your tether. It is not a failure to admit that your control will snap and you may do something dreadful if you do not have a break.

Baby battering is a tragedy whenever it occurs, and which of us who has had children and coped alone in the weeks after the birth has not come near to it, if we are honest? So no one should ever condemn a woman who loses control under great stress — she may have none of the understanding, or help, or resources which stay other women's hands.

But if you are alone all the time with the baby, with no cessation of care and no adult companionship, how can you avoid the break in control?

How to cope

The best thing to do, if the baby is crying and crying and you feel you can stand no more, is to put the baby down in a safe place — a cot or a pram for example — and go into another room and shut the door. Then you can pick up a pillow and scream blue murder into it, or say all that you want to say into it, and then if you still feel the need, thump the pillow until you are tired. That will take the physical energy of misery out of you without hurting the baby. Then if you can, go back and pick up the baby and try again to help it get over *its* misery. A baby can't beat hell out of a pillow. Try also to have something to eat, and a cup of tea or a hot drink; we often fail to realize how lack of food makes stress much worse.

You probably need to pour out your frustrations and problems to another adult. Local postnatal support organizations, such as the National Childbirth Trust Breastfeeding Counsellors and Postnatal Supporters, are always available by telephone. Don't be afraid to ring (see page 191).

There are many sources of advice and admonition which seem simply to add to the pressures at this time. Books may say, 'Keep up your appearance; you'll feel better if you look as good as you usually do.' 'Don't forget your husband — you're a wife before you're a mother and he mustn't feel left out in the cold.' 'Have a candlelit dinner once in a while to revive your romantic feelings.' 'Don't lose your identity — you're still the person you always were.' All this is good advice, for some, at some time. But since you both realize that you are *not* the same people, now that you have a baby, and that your lives have a new dimension — who is fast asleep in your arms or chuntering gently in the baby carrier as you wash up or go shopping — such advice sometimes sounds hollow. The thing you need is time: time to adjust, to come to terms with the new dimension, and to think. Ideally, a relaxed and lazy three months without pressures to be as you were, or to take up any pre-arranged threads; just getting to know the baby and gradually deciding priorities.

An acceptable period of vegetating is so valuable, and so rare. Given the chance to indulge in one, when a new baby arrives, why not revel in it? It may be a mixed comfort to know that the chance only really comes with your first child.

The mothers who talked so honestly about tiredness had something to say about coping with stress too.

Di 'When I feel I'm going to snap — and the baby might be at risk — because I *must* have a break from supporting her, I put her down safely and then go out of the room and do something to stop the unbearable tension. Finding another adult to talk to, having a good cry — anything to give me a chance to gather my wits and be calm again. It's important to *accept* that I'm tired — "OK, I'm tired, I can live with that!" '

Anne 'I try very hard not to get to that breaking point in the first place. When I see it coming and know the tension is building up, especially when my husband is away at sea, I get out with the baby. I sometimes take him to the Mums and Toddlers Group, even though he's only a few weeks old and years from being a toddler, or go to the shops or visit a friend. That usually stops the build-up of distress for both of us.

'When everything seems to be on top of me I make lists! I take five minutes to sit down and sort myself out. I make a list of all the things that I need and want to do, and then I score out everything that can wait. It ends up with one priority, and that's what I do.

'I'd say to every new Mum, "Get help, if you possibly can, even if it's for only an hour or two a week." Delegating some of the chores is something I needed to learn how to do, and the knowledge that someone, some other adult, is coming in quite soon is an enormous relief.'

Nicole 'When I know that if I hold my crying baby another minute I shall lose all control, I put her down in her bed or pram and sit down as far away from her as possible. I breathe deeply — more oxygen *does* help — and tell myself that it's not going to last. Maybe I go and have a shower, maybe I have a cry, away from the baby. Anything to let the tension out. Then I will safely go back and try again to comfort my daughter. It's good to have another adult around — but I don't yell for Tim, because he believes I *can* cope. That's flattering, but I don't want to hear it when I'm just about not to cope! I'd maybe telephone a special friend, who I know would understand and help me without soggy sympathy.'

Anna 'Everyone recognizes when the breaking point comes for them. I know this from my toddler group, and everyone deals with getting the tension out in their own way. It happened for me on one night when both my babies were crying and I could not stop them. I had to put them both down in their beds, and I went into my bedroom — Bob was away mountaineering — and climbed under the duvet and cried self-indulgently for about twenty minutes. Then I went back and coped again.

'Another friend of mine got to the same point, also in the middle of the night, and she simply put the baby down by her husband and said she was going out — and went. She walked around the village for about an hour, and then went back. But the baby was still crying, so she went out again for another half hour. Then she knew she could go back again and take it up. Her husband was very worried about her by then.

'In the end each of us had to come to terms with it, and live with it. Getting outside the house helps a lot. It stops you feeling trapped in a cage with the baby. It must be terribly hard in a flat. One thing I find helps a lot is to burst into song when things are difficult! I do that a lot. Singing is a great relaxation.'

Getting back into shape

Women vary a great deal over the speed and ease of getting back to shape after giving birth. Each person's basic metabolism is unique. In pregnancy some womens' bodies retain a lot of extra fluid, and others do not. Some women easily make more fat from their food, and others lose fat in pregnancy. So it is not surprising that you cannot tell before you have your baby how your own body will re-adapt to not being pregnant.

If you are one of the women who can walk out of the maternity hospital in the jeans you wore before you were four months' pregnant, then you are liable to catch the envious eyes of women who stay looking pregnant for weeks after giving birth. But whichever type of body you have, your stomach muscles have been stretched, and your ligaments have been softened by being pregnant, and you need exercise to return to your usual trim self.

Since everyone feels much better about life and living when they are physically fit, getting back to shape after birth is quite a priority. It is worth seeking out really good postnatal exercise classes, run by a qualified person — usually a physiotherapist or a yoga or dance teacher who knows the dangers of over-straining already stretched muscles. A routine of exercises, gentle at first but building up to a quite strenuous set after your six week postnatal check-up, will get you fit much quicker than you might expect.

Some women can work out their own set of exercises at home, and make sure they do them daily. But the majority of women find that in their new life with a new baby doing exercises is often the very first thing that gets left out. When you are tired, it's very difficult to believe that ten minutes' exercising will make you feel much better than ten minutes' rest and also make your rest and sleep more useful.

If you join a class for exercise sessions someone else tells you what to do, makes sure that you are doing it right, and encourages you to keep going. The company you are in is usually fun, and the music and breathing are refreshing. Many postnatal exercise classes run crèches for the babies of the women who come, and the classes don't last very long anyway.

One of the spin-offs of doing exercises for women who are breastfeeding their babies is that getting physically fit can help the milk production. It is often wrongly assumed that when you are feeding a baby, you need to rest a lot, drink a lot, and lead a very sedentary life. So women who are enjoying feeding their babies tend to put off getting back to fitness and allow the flab to stay for longer than it need. Other women who don't enjoy breastfeeding and long to have their bodies to themselves again rather than at the baby's beck and call, may fret about this and seek exercise classes as a way of escape. Both are usually very surprised to find that the breastfeeding is improved and much more acceptable as they get back into trim.

Mothers with new babies are always very busy, and can easily let their eating habits slip. It is so easy to snatch a sandwich or eat some chocolate when you have a free moment and can't face the effort of cooking yourself something nourishing. This is the quickest way to put on weight — and feel worse — when you probably want to *lose* weight and regain energy. Calorie-counting and *rapid* slimming diets are definitely not a good thing at this time, as you need feeding well. It's a good time to try a new approach, and make sure you feed for long-term health. Read about Food Combining (see page 189);

it is flexible, and you may find it helps a lot.

Getting fit again by eating sensibly and exercising helps to reduce any depression as you adjust to the new experience and demands after your baby arrives. Mothers who adopt babies have the same culture shock of total take-over of their lives by the baby, and need the same attention to their physical health. The only area they escape from is the need to do pelvic floor exercises after giving birth to a baby. Since getting your pelvic floor back to fine elastic tone makes you feel so much better, and improves your sex life, all women benefit from learning how to do the exercises, and should practise them daily. For those who have given birth, and maybe have had stitches to heal in their vaginas, pelvic floor exercises are a MUST, and good postnatal exercise classes will pay a great deal of attention to this. Also, in the long term, they will help you avoid the middle-age problems arising from having a slack pelvic floor, such as prolapse and stress incontinence.

If you have been very active in sports before you were pregnant, or all through your pregnancy, then getting back to fitness may not be too difficult. You may be surprised, though, at how much physical effort has happened during the labour, and how tired you may be after those few hours of spontaneous activity. After all, as I've heard women say, 'I wasn't rushing about during the birth, and most of the time I was in bed and still, so why do I feel so tired, or bruised, and shaky on my feet?' The reality is that your body works incredibly hard giving birth, and the uterus is the biggest and strongest muscle in the human body, and its energy and strength are a surprise to every woman who has a baby.

So care for yourself. Give your uterus and your stomach muscles time to rest and recuperate, and then gradually get them working well and smoothly again for the busy life ahead.

Going back to work

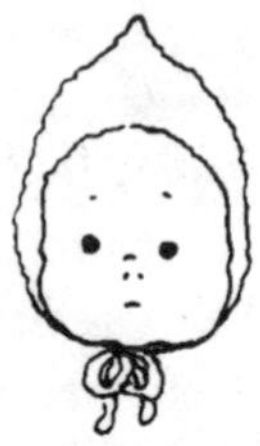

Without doubt, one of the most difficult problems new mothers have to face up to is whether or not to go back to work. If you have an interesting job with good prospects, and have run your own life for years, pregnancy will upset your plans for the future. It raises many questions: 'When should I stop work?' 'When can I return?' 'Shall I want to return?' 'Will my job be kept open for me?' 'If I don't return can we afford to live with a baby and without my salary?' 'If I am out of the workplace for a year or more, shall I slip behind everyone else?' 'Shall I be under a lot of pressure from my friends, relatives or neighbourhood either to return to work before I am ready, or not to return to work when I badly want to?' 'How do I feel about being totally dependent on my partner economically?'

With a first baby those are the questions which occur most often. It is only when the birth is past, and the baby is a reality, that the effect *on the baby* of your return to work becomes a reality too. You now have a new little person to consider, and it's a person with a very strong relationship with you, and a very definite place in your life. She or he may be quite different from the baby you imagined before it was born, and the strands of responsibility to yourself, to the baby's father and to the baby make a tangled skein which can take time to straighten out.

Be prepared for some unexpected changes in your ideas. You may have definite views about your intention to get back to work as soon as possible after the birth, and then find that your plans are unworkable.

Why your decision is important

What makes going back to work such an urgent issue for mothers? Ask new parents that and they will probably gaze at you in wonder that you even need to ask! 'Money,' most will say, 'To pay the mortgage,' or 'To do the best for my children,' or 'To keep my job open; if I stay away for a year to look after the baby, I shan't have a job to go back to!' or 'I should go mad cooped up at home with only the baby to talk to!'

Looking at these dispassionately, *of course* money is important, especially in days of fluid social change and job insecurity. The mortgage must be paid or the home goes; children must be fed and clothed; entertainment is a necessary part of our standard of living.

But 'doing the best for my children' is much less cut and dried. So often parents believe that clothes and toys, television and lots of food — 'things' — are what make children happy at home. If children, especially small children, were asked and able to organise their thoughts into coherent arguments, they would say something entirely different. More like, 'The same reliable old faces smiling at me each day,' or 'No loud, angry voices,' or 'Food when I'm hungry,' or '*Time* to get used to new places and people with Mum/Dad nearby,' or 'A feeling that I matter a lot to someone,' A longing for toys comes much later, usually through comparison with other children.

It is security of people that matters to children; places and possessions come second, a very long way behind. Only if people fail them do possessions become important as reliable 'friends'.

What frightens and unsettles children is restless unhappiness in adults. If parents are always trying to get away from their babies, to be 'free', the children sense this acutely. The result is often just what the parent wishes to avoid — the insecurity felt by the child makes him cling much more tightly to his parent to stop her or him going away! Answering this need for security of parental care is one of the hardest things for lively, active parents to accept. Bind the child closely to you and it will feel safe and move out into the wide world more quickly; push the child away and it will try never to let you out of sight.

It is difficult in a world of multiple distractions to retain a sense of time. The baby months and the childhood years seem unending when you are in them; looking back from the relative calm of middle age they were only a *short* part of your life. They are the days of laying foundations, for the children and for your relationship with them later on, which can either bring you endless joy and companionship, or acute heartache. They are *important* months, and deserve both parents' full attention. Decisions made now have long-term consequences.

A baby is in the best of all situations if both parents share the work and the fun. It *is* hard work — bringing up a family is a big job, and it is unrecognised by status or salary. Perhaps if parenthood carried an automatic performance-related pay structure men and women would take it seriously and study the terms and conditions offered them *before* they embarked on the career that parenthood is! The choice is there, but usually vague assumptions are made, and these blur the real importance of the needs of children.

Choices are particularly difficult for women. Balancing the demands of baby, partner, work, helpers, costs, health, friends and interests is like plate spinning. Women tend to be good at this, and can even manage to find a small amount of time for themselves! In some ways being at home with the baby is easier — you are your own boss and set your own rules and timetables. But for many it is hard to make that choice when it means less money coming in.

Different Options

If you do decide to continue working, in one form or another, there are a number of options to consider. I have spoken to many women who have found flexible and creative ways of combining a career with motherhood — even if it meant changing their original plans. What is most important is that you find a solution that is right for you and your baby.

One woman, Becky, is a teacher of music and travelled by train to the college where she taught three times a week. She is also a performer. She planned to take half a term off after her baby was born, to get it settled so that she could then take the baby with her by train three times a week and continue her teaching. When the baby was born she proved to be very alert and wideawake, resisted sleeping and so got overtired and became distraught. She needed, and demanded, a very quiet life, and was a very clinging baby. It was eighteen months before Becky was happily able to return to her teaching job, in spite of having help with the baby. *She*, the mother, was not happy to be away from her daughter until the baby was happy too. So she continued with her performing job, which could be managed, and her practising, and made her teaching wait.

Another woman, Teresa, is a lawyer, and her career is very important to her; there are not so many women barristers around and their places are quickly filled by ambitious men if they fade out for a time. She planned to return to work as quickly as she could after her baby was born. She firmly believed in breastfeeding and planned to have someone to look after the baby in the robing room at court, so that she could nip out in the intervals between cases to feed the baby. I suppose such a plan was bound to have difficulties, but Teresa managed it for a few weeks, and then decided that her career was so important for her peace of mind and happy motherhood that she gave up breastfeeding and had reliable permanent help to care for the baby at home while she was at court. She could afford it, and that was the right solution for her.

Firms employing women are gradually considering part-time working for women who have new babies, or flexi-time for the first few months after a baby has been born. Many women can adapt to this, and continue to work with part-time help from family or friends to care for their baby in their absence. Much more could be done along these lines to make it easier for women to be mothers and still keep up with their jobs. The loss of income when you give up your job is a real difficulty in these days of changed status and expectations.

For some women, returning to work is not what they want to do. They would prefer to have less money, and spend the first year or so of their baby's life at home as a parent rather than struggle to work for a sum which is paid straight out again to the child minder. It's a balancing act for every woman who is combining a baby with a job, and one to which there is no quick and simple solution. The answer to the problem will be different for each woman and family.

The options may appear easier if you are self-employed, and can arrange your work flexibly yourself. Women who work at home certainly have the advantage in one way — their time is their own to apportion. But they also have the disadvantage of having to concentrate on their work while the baby may wake or interrupt, and it sometimes seems that life would be much easier if they could go somewhere else and separate the two main interests of their lives.

Lyn is a potter, and she and her husband run a very successful business. When their first child was born Lyn intended to spend half of each day potting and helping on the selling side, and while the baby was very small it worked quite well. But as he grew and was mobile it became impossible to work with him playing around the clay, water, wheels and electricity. She had to give it up until he was old enough to go to playgroup in the mornings. When their second baby was born, she planned from the beginning to abandon any attempt at craft work until the days had a shape, with both children at playgroup or at school for set times.

Finding a child minder

It would be easy to say that women should settle down to a job of full-time motherhood for those years up to school age. But this is not the best thing for very many women, for whom the domestic life with a baby is very difficult to enjoy or find fulfilling.

There is no doubt that the baby needs a settled person, or persons, to look after it in the first year or two, so that it feels basically secure about life and living, and can develop independence. For the first few weeks the mother simply is life and security for the baby. For her, this is a personal growing time which she cannot avoid. But that growing time, a rite of passage into maturity, can begin to feel like a door closing into a trap for some women, and they need to know that there are options ahead. It is not necessarily the mother who is the best person to look after the growing baby once the first stability is reached. If she is fretting to get back to using her brain or her hands, is feeling lonely and shut-in at home, or has a baby with particular problems and no one coming in to share her extra difficulties, then she will not be happy. It may be much better for the baby as well as for her if she returns to work and leaves her baby in safe care while she is away.

One woman who is devoted to her two sons says with absolute honesty that she would have gone mad — and could have been a baby-batterer — if she had not been able to go back to at least part-time work by the time her babies were three to six months old. She says that she needed to work for *herself* and not for the money, because almost all she earns goes to the child minder anyway. In this she has the complete support of her partner who understands her need for mental stimulation and time for herself. If he had not agreed with her or did not understand and felt she should be at home all the time, then it would have been impossible for her to arrange their lives as she has done. I will tell their story in some detail as it shows up some of the problems of finding suitable child care help.

When their first son was four months old she began to look for a child minder. The Citizens Advice Bureau provided a list of registered child minders, and she went to the nearest one and spent the first week with her baby there. All seemed well, because while she was there the child minder sat with the children and played with them. She felt that her baby would get loving care and stimulation and she started back to work. But after a time the baby screamed whenever they went near the house and she realized that things were not going right for him. She discovered that the child minder was leaving the children alone while she did her own housework and attended to her own affairs. So she took her son away and started the hunt for another.

It was a long hunt; the next minder had a child of her own but the hours she could offer were not convenient and the baby had long waits for handing over. The next child minder she went to see was not yet registered; for some reason she felt that this woman was all wrong for looking after children. In fact she felt so very unhappy about the place that she decided not even to try it. Her happy ending came with a fourth child minder, who is wonderful with the babies and children for whom she cares, and devotes her whole day to looking after and interesting her charges.

You sometimes have to search very hard to find the person with whom you are happy to leave your child. It is essential to know that your baby is happy while you are away. If you know that the child may be miserable, then you spend all day thinking and worrying about it, and you get no joy from your own time at work. So nobody is happy or contented. Then you have to find another carer for your baby, or at least consider very carefully what you are getting out of your job, and whether you want to continue.

Your attitude to caring for your children may vary greatly from the first to the second or other children. No matter what you read in books, you cannot believe, just after your first baby is born, that the time will pass quickly until they start to go to school. The confusion of those first three months after childbirth makes the prospect of the next five years seem endless. If you are finding motherhood very hard to adjust to, one year looks like a life sentence, let alone five years. Yet looking back after that apparently endless year, you wonder where the time has gone. It has flown faster than you ever imagined it could.

With your second child you *know* how quickly the stages of babyhood change and how short a time each stage lasts. So you do not have the same feeling of endless nappy-changing and sleeplessness ahead of you. If you have also decided that this is going to be the last child you have, and your family is now complete, you may feel that the babyhood days are rushing by too fast and you almost want to slow them down. So seeking a child minder is every bit as important, because you know how important the baby's happiness is for these early years.

Whoever you go to for child minding, it is essential to sit down with them and talk about how you think a baby should be brought up and looked after. This person is going to be a major influence on your child, she is going to comfort the child when it bumps its head, is going to correct him when he has a disagreement with another child, is going to use words and ideas which will take root in your child's mind. It is very necessary that you and the child minder understand each other's priorities, and that you share the same outlook on how children grow and develop best.

Staying at home

Your instinct about your child is very strong, and you need to trust it. Whenever you have a decision to make about what to do, take as careful a look as you can at your baby, and decide what is best for him or her. With any luck that will be what is best for you too. Sometimes that's the most difficult decision to take.

Nancy, for instance, felt instinctively that her baby needed to have her at home all the time in her first year, so she stayed at home in her little house in Cambridge. She found that she was the only mother in the street who didn't take her child to a crèche and go on to an intellectual job; what's more, all the other women were not slow to tell Nancy how much they disapproved of her decision to stay at home, and what a lot of harm she was doing by depriving her baby of the company of other babies. So she had a hard time. The result, however, has been wholly good, because her child is friendly, balanced, integrated, and clever. Her instinct for her child was worth trusting.

It seems that these days it is quite hard for women to justify their desire to stay at home when they have a baby, and *not* go out to work. Actually to enjoy being a home-based mother full-time is regarded as rather strange. Yet from the baby's point of view, to be cared for by a contented mother, who finds life fulfilling because of your existence, is a very happy state of affairs. Many women, if they are honest, would love to be able, financially, to stay at home when their babies were growing and enjoy caring for and getting to know their own children really well. The important thing is that those who feel this is the way for them should be able to do so.

One of the things that young women worry about is that they may 'lose their identity' when they become mothers. You may find yourself in a battle between self-realization and selfishness. Each woman has to resolve this for herself, and honesty is often very hard. But if selfishness is really being considered, then you would probably be wise to give maximum time and attention to settling your baby securely into life in his or her first year. This will help your toddler to branch out into independence with confidence. That way, you get far more rewards of personal freedom in the later years!

For single parents the problems of decisions on where your baby will be cared for when you return to work are the same — but the options are narrowed. First there is probably *no* option to remain at home with your baby, and second your resources are certainly halved, with no adult available to share the money-earning and home care. This means that your choice of alternatives is limited by the job you do — and the stress you carry is much greater. Your need for support from family, friends, society and organisations is pressing. Whatever the reasons are for the single parent bringing up a baby alone, she or he needs the best neighbourly help that can be given. Ostracism or disapproval only makes life harder for the baby, and it is the baby's welfare which should matter to everyone concerned, whether individuals or government organisations.

Adapting to life with a baby is hard work enough when two parents share the responsibility; it is *much* more difficult for one alone.

Interview with Phillipa

Phillipa and husband Harry live in a city and both work in advertising. They have one son, Oliver, who is two years old. Phillipa stayed at home for over six months after Oliver was born, but then was ill herself and needed a period in hospital. After that she went back to work part time. Harry had some months out of work so this was necessary as well as being what she wanted.

Q. Were you always sure you would return to work soon after Oliver's birth?
Phillipa 'I wasn't sure. My first decision was *not* to go back. A new baby is so small, and must be properly looked after. At first, coming out of full-time work, I loved looking after Oliver and being at home. But after some months I did miss the stimulus of working, and had to face up to what is really a major decision. I'd never work full time, I think, but part time is right for me. It would have been harder if I definitely didn't want to work, but had to because of finances. For us that became the case *after* I'd decided to go back to part-time work.'

Q. What are the options in child care for working mothers in a city?
Phillipa 'I found there were about six:
1. One-to-one child care at home, either live-in or live-out, depending on the hours you work. Preferably live-in, especially if I work unstructured hours. It's not cheap.
2. Child minding in someone else's home; registered child minders can take up to three children, with extensible hours. I would have to take and fetch.
3. Nurseries, which are really extended playgroups with fixed hours, taking babies from months onwards.

4. Nanny-sharing. We would share with another couple, either with both children at one of the homes, or worked around families with different age group children. In that case it could be, for example, mornings with Oliver at our home, and afternoons fetching the other families' children from school etc. This is becoming more and more popular, and the cost would be like the live-out carer, but shared equally. It's a flexible scheme, entirely dependent on finding the right person, which can be very difficult.
5. State nurseries, which are cheaper but take many more children. There aren't many of them and they can be a long way from where you live and work.
6. A crèche. Some offices and businesses provide crèches for their employees, but these are very rare at present. It would be marvellous if more provision of this sort were developed, because the baby would be within reach in case of need, and mothers wouldn't worry so much about whether the baby was happy and alright.'

Q. Which did you choose?
Phillipa 'The first — but almost by accident, because Harry had a cousin who wanted a job after leaving school. She came to stay and help me when I was in hospital, and after I came out and wasn't allowed to lift Oliver for some months. She was such a success that she stayed on with us while she found another job training for working with small children. We now have a working arrangement with her which we hope will suit us both as she gets her training. We were very lucky; when she was away for a while helping another mother with a new baby I realised how difficult it could have been, as Oliver didn't settle at all well at the nursery school we tried.'

Q. How did you find the nursery school?
Phillipa 'By personal recommendation in my case. Libraries are places where anyone can find lists of registered child minders, and nurseries in your area. It's *very* important to find

the right place for your baby, because if you don't feel 100 per cent content with where he is, you are worrying all the time and feel guilt-ridden at not being with him or her. Then of course you don't work well, and it's *so* difficult. When Oliver was unhappy and I had to leave him each day in tears, and fetch him in tears, it was devastating. I decided to take him away from that nursery, and the minute I had made the decision he suddenly changed and ran into the school happily each day! Aren't children wonderful, after all the churning emotions — or was it because he sensed I was happy to be stopping him going there and he instinctively knew things were different? Who knows?'

Q. Are there any other alternatives to paid help?
Phillipa 'Some couples manage to do a complete role-reversal. The mother goes out each day to work in full-time employment or training, and the father stays home and is a house husband. It is still socially less acceptable, although it was the only solution for many families in the depression of the 1930s, and again in this recession. It can work well if the father feels good about it. But lots of men feel that cooking and cleaning is not very manly work, or interesting (lots of women feel that way too!) and if they are restless it causes a lot of friction.

'Then there are family helpers, and this must be the only way for so many women who go back to work because they must, or badly want to, and can't possibly pay for carers because either they don't earn enough, or they have no room for such help. In days past grandmothers often cared for the baby grandchild while the mother worked; but these days grandmothers are often working themselves, and want lives of their own outside the home. There are some male nannies too, now, because unemployment is such a problem.'

Q. How do you feel about the care of Oliver now?
Phillipa 'I know my child is happy, and that's good. But there

are times when I feel pulled three ways — mother, wife and wage earner. I like my work and I know I'm good at it, but there are times when I work at home and there's a crossover; someone else is influencing my small son, when his mind is so interesting and receptive, and I almost feel envious of the child carer, because *I'd* like to stop working and play with him!

'Some mothers say they are sure they are better mothers for being at work. When they are at home it is very much one-to-one with the child and is quality time, but they know that would suffer if they had to spend their home time doing all the domestic chores. They have to earn enough money to pay for domestic help as well as child caring. I find it *very* irritating to realise how low motherhood is rated in our time. When I'm asked what I do now, I say "I'm a mother, and I do some work outside my home as well." That's my answer.'

Q. What would make the whole thing easier?
Phillipa 'State provision of really good child minding would make all the difference to so many *many* women with families — and it could be a marvellous way of giving all babies some early education. It could be a way of breaking the 'cycle of deprivation' for families in need too. But I can't see the government taking that on, can you? Or any future government, for years and years. The next best thing would be lots of available domestic help — like the 'home-helps' of the 1950s and 1960s. You are so much more on your own now, especially with the extended family often far away. The whole age range of child-bearing is changing too; lots of women are not starting their families until well into their thirties, and will be much older grandparents if their children do the same. Right now, young mothers want the choice — to stay at home if they think that's best for their baby, or use flexible working time to earn money and keep skills.'

Q. Have you thought of having an au pair to help at home?
Phillipa 'No. An au pair is rather different, because girls from another country come to learn English and live in a family almost as an extra teenager. They have to have pocket money and a good deal of free time. They cannot be used for heavy housework, or take on sole responsibility for children. So in a way an au pair is an *extra* burden because you have to take on the welfare and care of a young foreigner.'

Sharing the burden

Talking with Phillipa and other mothers about their difficult decisions over returning to work, it became clear that many partners were much happier when the burden of earning money was shared. Many said that fathers were more willing to help with chores once the mothers returned to part-time or full-time work.

This is relevant mainly to the first child, because with a second or subsequent baby it is *much* more difficult for a woman to make satisfactory child care arrangements. At the same time the financial strain on the wage-earner is heavier, and this can be a cause of strain between the parents (which affects the children too). It is important to talk about it and understand each other's worries and tiredness.

Margaret, mother of twins after two earlier children, said, 'I went back to work, teaching, when the twins were about two-and-a-half, and were in nursery school. Things became easier then. My husband felt that I was sharing in the financial strain of supporting four kids — which the twins had made extra stressful — and I enjoyed doing something outside the home. He suddenly became adept at washing and ironing, and even cooking which he had *hated* doing before!'

Each family has to work out the best way for them. The old 'middle class' pattern of the father going out to work and the mother staying at home is a thing of the past. This is one of the greatest changes in society over the last half century. The sisterhood of working mothers has widened and class barriers have come down. The only danger is that the people who may suffer are the children. In the first year, when they are babies, the foundations of their security are being laid.

THE BABY'S FIRST YEAR

Introduction

All parents look for landmarks in the baby's growth and progress. Some sort of general guidelines may be a help towards understanding what skills the average baby develops as he or she moves through the first year. But it must always be borne in mind that an 'average' is a middle between widely divergent ends. To expect your baby to do anything at exactly the same time as any other baby is a mistake. It is only when a baby learns a skill a great deal earlier or later than many other babies that you need to and look for reasons.

I knew one baby who didn't talk at all until he was over four years old, although he was perfectly responsive and alert and appeared to understand what his parents and siblings said and did. His mother and father were unworried for a year or two — they knew that some children are very slow to talk. But then they began to be seriously concerned — was their son deaf? Was he mentally defective? Then one morning at family breakfast the little boy was gazing at the Cornflakes packet and suddenly opened his mouth and said 'Absolutely delicious'. He was reading! Like many very bright babies he had realized very early that if he pointed at something, or nodded or yelled he could get what he wanted without all the bother of talking.

That was an extreme case; but many modern parents worry greatly if their children are not progressing as fast as they think should be the case, or as the child next door is.

It is much more comfortable and less stressful if you can look at your baby and see whether she or he is eating well, and sleeping well, and responding to you in the way that babies can, by smiles and gurgles and body movements. Keeping a record is interesting, and when the baby is an older child there is great interest in seeing how they behaved in infancy.

Try to keep a record of the interesting or unusual things that your child may do and funny things he or she may say. They slip out of mind so quickly if they are not written down. Older children enjoy looking back on them. Photographs help, and home videos are of endless interest to the children concerned. All of these reinforce a child's sense of identity and the family network.

After a few weeks

As a baby grows — and they grow very fast in these early months — he or she develops other needs than eating and being comforted and asks for new responses. When a baby gets used to the feelings of digestion and settles on one or another feeding routine, it seems to be free to start taking an interest in what is going on around it in the wider world. Usually the first really interesting thing outside its own sensations and internal needs is its mother.

With each of my children there has been a lovely moment, somewhere between two and six weeks old, when the baby has suddenly *seen* my face, rather than just looking at it, only a foot above its own face as it was feeding. The sudden surprise of focusing on someone else's eyes and recognizing a person is enough to stop the baby sucking, and make it fall away from the breast or the bottle with an indescribable expression of wonder and delight. Such a milestone gives a great boost to the mother's confidence. It is delightful when a baby laughs at you, with sheer pleasure at seeing your face. From then on it wants to see and recognize you more, and needs to know you are around. It goes on to include other adults in the family and other siblings.

Since it is growing in awareness of the world around it, the baby may now experience boredom and loneliness if it is left alone and in one position for a long time. Imagine how boring it would be to find yourself lying on your side in bed facing a wall, and for some reason quite unable to turn over when you wanted to. That's what many an older baby cries about when they have woken after sleeping in a carrycot or crib. Once realized it is easy to help this boredom by putting pictures at the level of the baby's head beside its bed, at a distance where it can see, or by fixing up mobiles as it grows to want moving things to watch.

When awake, babies enjoy being placed in some safe position — in a baby chair or bouncer, or propped in a chair with cushions — so that they can see people around and watch movement.

For many babies, parallel with their growth in movement and experiments in using their arms and legs, comes frustration. The more awake and aware the baby is the more frustrated it will be at not yet being able to do the things it naturally wants to do. Very early on the baby may focus on a coloured ball strung across its pram or cot, watch it, talk to it in baby noises, laugh at it — and then try to touch it. It is probably too far away, and the baby's movements are not yet well enough co-ordinated to make touching it possible, and that is frustrating. Help is called for from a parent who will learn what that cry of anger is for. It's probably for comfort too.

I have never had a 'gifted' child, one who is heading for membership of Mensa from the start, and I have been grateful for that! Such babies' minds race ahead of their physical abilities, and they need so much attention and stimulation to ease their frustration and feed their eagerness to learn, that it is a tremendous job being a parent to them. Even perfectly average children sometimes want to stand before they can sit safely, run before they can stand steadily, and suffer agonies of frustration because they don't have the language to explain what they want. Parents' skills of understanding and interpreting simply mushroom in response. Everyone knows how fathers and mothers can understand what a very young baby is implying by its behaviour, and how an older baby's first words may be unintelligible to everyone except its parents, who know at once what it is saying. The parents of gifted children need extra support and help to keep pace with the demands upon them.

All babies learn fast, and it is fun to know how to teach new skills even to very young babies. I have seen a mother who talks to her three-month-old baby, and when she has the baby's attention focused on her face, she gently puts her tongue out a little bit at the baby, followed by a little murmuring talk. She does this three or four times, and surprise surprise, the baby then puts out its tongue a little, copying exactly what its mother is doing. Learning by imitation starts right from the beginning of awareness, not only with physical skills like nodding and smiling, and later on clapping and pointing and so on, but with more subtle mimicry such as of tones of voice, responses, and physical attitudes.

There are also many subconscious things that a baby senses very quickly and acutely. If a mother is tense, or anxious, or afraid, there is no way that she can hide this from a baby. In simple things this is swiftly apparent; if a baby dislikes being dressed, and screams when a jumper is put over its head, the mother may be nervous about the coming battle whenever she has to dress him, and the baby knows from her anxiety what is to come, and is tensed up ready for the battle! One way out of that particular problem is to try other ways of dressing him, make games of it, and definitely swap to cardigans if you can until the putting-things-over-the-head fear disappears into the past and fades from the baby's memory.

If a baby senses moods over everyday things like being dressed or fed, or knows at once if you are going out for the day and really want him to sleep so that he is not too tired, the baby will respond to your anxiety by being unable to sleep at all. Then how much more will even a very young baby react to friction between parents or among other family members, and the real unhappiness they sense in the person whose arms they are in. When violence is involved and fear is communicated to the baby, it lives a life of tension.

The long-term results of such emotions in the baby life of individuals are only slowly being fully understood or stressed. In our society, where babies are taken for granted far too often, unintentional harm can be done by simple ignorance of the fact that the baby learns from *everything* going on around it.

At six months

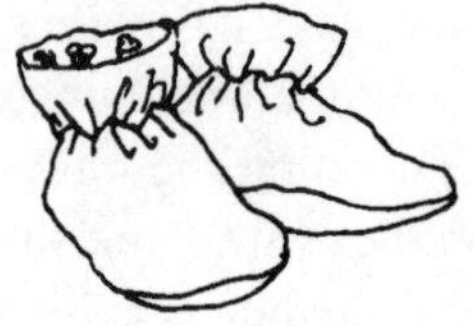

Most new parents find that their lives get much more interesting and rewarding as their baby grows older month by month. My husband could never work up much enthusiasm for very tiny babies — except for his own. And even they, miraculous and unbelievable as they were at birth, were nowhere near as interesting to him as his work, until they began to be active. In his own words, babies should be born at six months old! Once they started to sit up and try to talk, and even more when they learned to move about, he found them more and more interesting each day. Other men I know have a greater delight in tiny babies, and they may find their babies more difficult when they start to crawl and walk and take an interest not just in toys but in tools and possessions too. It all depends on individual man's temperaments and priorities.

For most, the baby at six months is great. He or she can sit up, maybe propped with cushions until balancing is sorted out. They take an interest in everything they can see, so mobiles and pram beads and anything moving within their range of sight are distracting and worth their attention. Going out in the pram or push chair is always interesting, because people and flowers and shops and cars are everywhere, and most babies find outings a very good use of time. It's a pity we cannot remember clearly what it was like to be pushed along, warmly tucked up in a reasonably comfortable container, with plenty to look at, an adult constantly there to respond to our needs. And if it all got too much, the chance to drop off to sleep where one was, rocked comfortably and with plenty of steady noise to lull one off.

Noise

Steady background noise is one thing; sudden loud noises are quite another. Babies jump out of their skins if an aeroplane screams by overhead, or a car backfires, or thunder suddenly cracks very close, or a car stops nearby with its radio blaring loud. They find this frightening, and need quite a lot of soothing to recover from their fright. Parents rapidly learn what noises scare their babies, and become very sensitive to the sort of sounds that babies hear. An adult's hearing is very selective, and each person has their own list of noises which irritate or distress them. Babies' lists are usually rather different, and it is very useful to work out bit by bit what noise it is which makes your baby laugh, or cry, or perk up with interest. Sometimes babies who are very musical are particularly sensitive to noise of all sorts. This can be hard to live with, especially if you have neighbours whose noise sensitivity is very different from the baby's, and your child cannot sleep unless there is quiet around her. Neighbourly relations can get very strained.

When our first baby was born we were living overseas in a desert. It was very hot, and our next-door neighbours owned a pair of macaws. Their bungalow was about 30 yards away from ours, and when our baby was asleep in her pram I used to put her on our balcony in the shade, where there was a breeze to help her to keep cool. Our neighbours had no children, and never bothered to move from room to room in their bungalow in order to speak to each other — they shouted across the rooms instead. And every time they shouted, the macaws would screech in competition. The noise was unbelievable, and if it happened when our baby was on the balcony it often woke her up with a start, and she would cry with fright.

I was very young and didn't know whether to complain and ask them to change their ways, or whether that would be rude. But I was rendered quite speechless when one day they came across to our bungalow and asked me to keep our baby in the house because they were disturbed by the noise of her crying!

Babies can learn to ignore noise, especially if it is continuous, or happens regularly, such as living next to a railway or an airport. It is the sudden, unexpected noise that frightens or wakes them.

Movement

Some six-month-old babies are beginning to want to move around, and will roll over or reach in all directions to try to get the thing that has caught their eye, or the person they want to touch or have lift them up. The first time they roll over may be a big surprise and they may cry with the shock; the temptation then is to lift them up and cuddle them and make a great fuss, probably because *you* are frightened by the baby's cry, and may be afraid that he or she is hurt. It helps the baby to learn that rolling over is a useful thing to do, and really doesn't hurt. Reassure and encourage the baby with a stroke and sounds of admiration for its skill! You want the baby to learn to be mobile and resilient, so, provided there really is no hurt and the baby is in a safe place, then help it to learn that movement is survivable.

Of course, if you have left the baby on your bed and it rolls over and falls off on to the floor, that is a different thing entirely, and should be taken very seriously indeed. Accidents happen so quickly, and can be very long-term in their effects. Forethought is necessary. Most accidents happen because the parent does not realize that the baby is at the stage of ability which makes the accident likely.

A baby's rolling skill can be amusing. I remember being at a meeting where there were two babies of about six months old. At one time during a discussion session these two babies spotted each other across the room. For a while they just looked at each other, and then they each started to roll over towards each other. It took them about half an hour, but they got to each other in the end, in the middle of the floor, and spent a long time investigating each other with eyes and fingers and by making noises. They totally stole the show as all the adults were fascinated to see these two exploring their own world, at slow speed, and at floor level.

Seeing

Six-month-old babies' reactions are slow; they take time to look at new things, and take in a new feeling or taste or sound. Adults often find a baby's stare unnerving. They can look at you for a long time without blinking, and grown-ups have forgotten how to do this without feeling uncomfortable and forced to respond in some way. When a baby really looks at you, let it look, and don't feel uncomfortable — it needs to take its time absorbing the shape of your face, or your hand, and deciding whether it likes this new shape or not. If you smile, move slowly and talk gently, it will be more reassuring to the baby than sudden movements, or tickling, or sudden noises. Your face needs to be familiar to your baby, and new people coming in must be known and absorbed before the baby can feel safe to respond to them. People who know about babies usually ignore them when they enter a room, and allow the baby plenty of time to get used to the sight and voice of the new person before they make overtures to it. The visitor who rushes at the baby when entering a room, or picks it up immediately, or bends over the pram making gooing noises, is likely to be rewarded with a poker face, a trembling lip, or a cry of dislike. Babies, like dogs, should be allowed time to make the first overtures themselves, and should never be rushed.

Once again it is worth thinking about what adults look like to a baby. To start with, an adult looks *enormous*. To prove this, try lying down on the floor flat on your back, as a baby would be if he were kicking on a rug, or sitting up at six months. Look up at your partner or friends or family in the room. It is a strange angle from which to see them, but it is the normal way that your baby sees grown-ups. Lying there, if someone walks towards you, or steps over you, you feel very vulnerable, and wonder whether they will step on you or trip over you. So does the baby. Even a dog or a cat looks threatening and large. If an adult bends above you as you lie on the floor, they tower over you; and if they smile they are all teeth, and floppy hair hanging down around their face. That's how you appear to a baby when you bend above it.

Amusement

This is about the easiest age to take a young baby anywhere. They are still small enough to sleep in a carrycot, and established enough to be fed at longer intervals and sleep for longer regular periods. They are probably on mixed feeding, and used to tasting a little bit of this and a little bit of that, but not yet feeding themselves and getting in an awful mess doing it. They're interested and alert, but not as vulnerable as they will be a few months later when they are walking. Because they are trying to move and using their muscles sitting up they get more tired and sleep longer at night. They have a stronger grip on life.

This is a very good age to take a baby on holiday, whether it is for days out by car or train, or going to stay with friends or relatives, or going further afield. Overseas travel is easy if you are still breast-feeding your baby, because you do not have to worry about the water supply in the country you visit (the mother digests the water before it ever reaches the baby, and she will be very careful if the local supply is suspect) and tinned or powdered foods are safe and easy to carry with you.

At six months a baby may very easily become bored unless he or she has new things to do and see and hear. Sometimes new parents do not realize that the baby's reasons for crying change round about this age, and many mothers feel rejected if the baby doesn't want to be fed, or rocked to sleep, or have its nappy changed, or be soothed. It may be saying that it doesn't know what it wants, but it wants something to change! Most adults know that feeling — you're sick of the old routine and want something to brighten up your life. For a baby, giving a zip to life is relatively easy; a new brightly coloured toy, even if it's just a painted wooden spoon from the kitchen, a first look at the television with those endless moving colours and shapes, going out for a walk, being picked up to be shown the pictures on the walls, being given a piece of tough scrumply paper to investigate, or a rattle or bell, playing peep-bo with an adult beside you — there are a hundred ways to change a baby's life.

Teething

It is at this age too that some babies' first bout of teething happens. Pain in their gums is strange and scary to a baby, and many of them find pain quite intolerable, especially if it is in their head. You can tell if their gums are the source of the pain by gently rubbing them with your finger; sometimes there is a red part which is tender, and sometimes the baby has one bright red cheek which shows which side the tooth is developing. It is the pressure of the tooth growing up through the gum which causes the pain. Once the tooth has erupted out of the gum the pain goes away. Some babies want to gnaw something to relieve the discomfort — their fingers, your fingers, a toy or a bone. Some bang their heads in distress, and if they do this you have to be careful to pad the bars of their cots or make sure they are not near to sharp edges of furniture.

Relief of the pain is difficult at this tender age, but there are useful preparations to soothe the gums which can be bought at the chemist and rubbed on with your finger, and these can help a lot. Teething may be a baby's very first experience of pain, other than inoculations or accidental bumps and bangs. It is something new and unpleasant which doesn't go away quickly and it takes some imagination to realize fully what an effect it can have on your baby's mood for quite a long time.

Baby-sitters

It is round about this time that it is wise to introduce the baby to some reliable baby-sitters, if you haven't already done so. If you never go out or leave the baby with a third person, the baby becomes dependent on having the same handling from the same person at the same time each day or night, and finds it more and more difficult to get on well with strangers. This can be over-protective, and restrictive for the parents as well as the baby. Of course you must be very careful about whom you trust to look after your baby while you are out. You may prefer only to rely on a relative whom the baby knows, or a friend; you may prefer to pay a baby-sitter with whom you have made a contract which gives you more control.

Whoever you choose to baby-sit for you, it is wise to start slowly, for short times and not very often, until you are sure the baby is fine while you are away. If the baby is unwell you would probably decide to stay with it, unless there were urgent reasons for going away, and you were very sure of the competence of the baby-sitter.

In these days of widening knowledge of child abuse, you would also want to check that the baby had been properly and well treated while you were not there, with no bruises or jitters to point to things having gone wrong. A useful pointer is how any baby responds to the arrival of the baby-sitter once they are known. If the baby smiles and asks to be held by the person, then probably all is well. If the baby does not want to go to the person, find a new baby-sitter.

The same watchful care is needed if you are going back to work and finding a child-minder. The baby will not be able to tell you in words how she is enjoying, or not enjoying, the time with the child-minder. But she or he will tell you very plainly by their behaviour.

At nine months

From six months onwards the baby's abilities widen every day. Milestones arrive and pass at different times, depending on the temperament of each child. My mother-in-law was very aware of this when she reminisced about her two elder sons. The eldest was restless, lively, energetic, and never stayed still unless he was fast asleep — an exhausting baby to bring up. The next son was quite different in temperament, and she remembered him sitting up in the pram at nine months old, watching his elder brother rushing around and refusing to get into the pram to be pushed, with a look of amazement and wonder on his face, as if he was thinking 'Why on earth is he running when he could so easily be sitting in the pram with me and letting someone else do the work?'

Mobility

Some babies will sit for hours on the floor or in a playpen, exploring their toys and looking around, listening to music on the radio, and remain perfectly happy. Others hate to be left in a room on their own, and cry to be picked up whenever their mother or father goes into another room. They want to be with company, where the action is, and entertaining themselves is nowhere near as good as being entertained by the actions of their parents.

Not very long after six months some babies start to try to get around on their own, and they find all sorts of different ways of doing it. By nine months many babies can move about the room, either by shuffling along on bottoms and legs, by rolling or pushing backwards, or by crawling on hands and knees. The first time a baby manages to push itself up on to its knees by its arms, it is often astonished, and can find it difficult to let itself down again. It's a funny moment, for everyone except the baby, who may cry with fear at being stuck, and again when the strain is too much and it flops down to the floor again. But the second time it knows how to flop, and in no time at all the baby is mobile.

This is when a new sort of fun begins. Before you have a baby you get used to putting things on the floor, knowing that they will stay there until you want to use them again. But when your baby starts to crawl around everything is interesting to her or him, and a book, a cup, a bag of knitting, or the paper seem like new toys and just right for investigation. So you very soon get used to moving all your adult activities up higher, out of reach of small fingers. Any precious china, and ornaments, and records or tapes have to be stored above reach also, unless you would prefer a life of worry and rushing to stop the baby all the time. Remember that this is a temporary phase, like all other stages in a child's life; it will not be long, only a few months.

Once the child understands what 'No' means, and will learn which things are not to be touched, then the precious things can be brought back to their places again. But at this early stage it is wiser to make your rooms places where the baby can crawl safely and without causing you anxiety. This avoids stress.

Babies test most things for interest first with their hands, and then by their mouths. It seems at first as though everything goes into their mouths and is tasted and chewed. They learn fast — anything which tastes nasty is not tried again. Almost all babies try earth and grass when they first start crawling in a garden, and spit them out again with a comical look of disgust. Their mouths also act as a useful extra hand when they need both arms and hands to get around with, and if they find something they want to take with them — a small toy or a spoon, or a piece of paper — they pop that thing in their mouths while they crawl to the place they want to get to.

This is a source of worry to parents, because so many things can be dangerous to a baby. You don't want to make the baby nervous, or inhibit the natural curiosity by which small animals learn. But nor do you want the baby to find out the hard way with things as dangerous as electricity or fire. By looking ahead you can avoid most disasters: fireguards should be in place before a baby crawls; electric power points should have safety covers; pins, needles, scissors, knives, medicines, pills should all be well out of the baby's reach, or locked up. Then you have peace of mind, and are free of anxiety about avoidable accidents.

That doesn't stop you having eyes like hawks in other people's houses! Parents bring up children in many different ways, and some appear to take risks that others would not take. Families whose children have grown up sometimes forget how different life was when their children were small, and households where there are no young children simply do not see the dangers in their homes. So it is never too early to start teaching your baby that there are things which must not be touched, just so that they are safer in the world outside your own home.

Discipline

'No' is such an emotive word. It can be said with authority, or without conviction, and small children will quickly learn which tone of voice is which. It can be said with alarm, which frightens the baby, or anger which frightens the baby even more — there is nothing so terrifying as looking up at that towering adult above you who is wearing a furious face. Try it and see.

The best tone, if you can manage it, is a cool firmness, and babies very soon know that tone and although they may try again and again to do the thing you are saying 'no' to, they know the restriction and will learn. Once learned, without fear or pain, you have established the authority for safety which stands the baby in good stead throughout childhood. But calm firmness is often very difficult to achieve, especially if you are tired or busy, have several children to look after, or are not well yourself, or have other anxieties. Most parents fail time and time again, and do react to dangers with anger or a slap.

Since slapping or shaking a baby gives pain, and may cause irreversible damage, the baby will be very frightened and will cry or scream and take a long time and a good deal of skill to calm and soothe back to happiness again. You, as an adult mother or father, always feel bad after losing your temper with a baby or a small child, and when you are feeling this way you may react even more harshly. You are angry with yourself and feel guilty, trying to justify what you have done, and it all spills out over anyone or anything which happens to be near. Most babies are amazingly resilient, and *do* get over an isolated incident, but it may take quite a lot of getting over. The trouble is that the very person — the baby's father, or mother — to whom she or he would naturally turn for help and comfort when in difficulty or distress, has been the one who hurt and frightened them, and that is confusing in the baby's mind. The baby would naturally avoid anything which hurt it, and yet this is the big person from whom up till then it has sought shelter in trouble.

After a lapse of anger when you may have been cross or rough with the baby, it is important to tell the baby that you are sorry, and as you soothe it when it is crying, to explain to it just *why* you lost control. The very act of talking it all out to the baby is healing, and helps you to understand what you are feeling and what strains you are under.

That goes particularly for fathers, because they are the sex which doesn't tend to talk so easily about their stresses. The strong silent male, the tough Macho male, the quiet martyr male, prides himself on not showing gentle tenderness, and feels dreadful when he is irritated beyond bearing and breaks out into violence. Many women — not all — can have a big cry and pour it all out verbally to a confidante they can trust. If only men could do the same it would be such a help, and might avoid the volcanic build-up of stress which can erupt and cause much damage.

It is when the baby starts to be mobile at this age that space becomes much more important to a new family. So many families live in flats or a few rooms, or at worst just one room, and it may have been possible to fit in the baby while it was more or less confined to a carrycot or pram. But now the baby is moving around, it is much more difficult for everyone to have space of their own.

The problems of living at very close quarters with your own children are quite enough to cope with, without having very close neighbours above and below and no outdoor space to escape to. It is no wonder that the modern problems of baby battering and abuse of children have risen so sharply — parental stress and living in housing which is unfit for families are often to blame. Parents who live in inner cities, in modern high-rise blocks, and bring up their children with love and care, well deserve the highest praise and admiration. They are the heroes of our times.

Your one-year-old

Life with baby is now quite definitely easier than it was a year ago. For one thing you know your baby now, very well indeed. And you and he or she have survived a great deal together. You share an equality of learning, for the baby knows you too now, very well indeed. He knows other people, a varying circle according to where you live and what sort of lifestyle you maintain, but he knows none so well as his parents, who have been his support and his anchor during these crucial first twelve months.

If the baby is happy with his learning so far, if he knows for certain that his parents are his trusted friends as well as the source of food and comfort and authority, then he will be ready to widen his interests. He will be paying more and more attention to the world beyond the cot, the pram, the living room, the house. Already crawling is a mastered skill for most babies, and some will be standing or walking.

Babies of this age begin to show how much they like and need the company of other children. They respond to playmates with delight. Once again, each child is different; some need to start with just one other baby, in the safety of their own home; others can feel happy in a group of children.

A little time taken to get the baby used to having other babies or older children around pays off wonderfully. Often it's a great help to have some much older children around, who like babies and will play with them without competition for toys. Baby humans develop possessiveness quite naturally! Home is the safest place for small children to learn about babies and how to play without teasing, and for babies to learn about older children and begin to copy the way they move and behave. The more they are used to other children in their own home, even for quite short periods, the easier it will be for them to adapt to playgroup, crèche, or kindergarten, and, eventually, school.

Children certainly need other children for interest, stimulation and identification. Their place in their own family is important, and parental skills about mixes of personality are vitally important. Family strains and misunderstandings have been the theme for books and plays and novels and learned treatises since the year dot. It is always more dramatic when relationships go wrong, but much sorrow and anxiety can be avoided if parents of new babies get to know their characters well from the start, and as they grow, teach them understanding of other children and of the situations that they will get into.

Older babies also need parental encouragement to try new things. The difference in temperament between children in the same family is a constant wonder to many parents, and each child will need differing help and encouragement. This makes the parenting job much more interesting and absorbing. How to give enough enthusiasm to a very nervous toddler about taking his first step alone, how to restrain the confident sister of that same toddler from overwhelming him with help — these are the kinds of variety which are constantly present in a family.

From babyhood on, most children learn best by praise and admiration from adults they trust. Once in the habit of expecting a toddler or a small child to be 'naughty' and do everything wrong, you fall quickly into the commands-and-obedience pit, and it is very hard indeed to change the negative atmosphere between parents and child. It's much easier, and a great deal more fun, to be a step ahead in understanding what your child is ready for. Encourage him or her to try to do something new and expect them to succeed. Always give praise for effort and response. That habit can stick, to everyone's future benefit.

The baby is now beginning to work out how to react to the environment around him. There has been physical stability and growth in the past year; then awareness of the world outside the baby's own body, and the mother who has been the only security; then interest in colours and movement and sounds in the home where he or she lives, and the wider world outside the home.

Now that the baby can move around — with a lot of fear and unsureness to begin with, and then increasing confidence — you can actually watch your child's mind working out how to achieve changes that are desirable, rather than just accepting the situation. For example, if a brightly coloured toy is on the edge of a low table and the baby wants it, he may crawl across to the table and pull himself up — only to find himself on the wrong side of the table and unable to reach the toy. Earlier he might have become frustrated and then given up, but at round about a year old he may stand and ponder the problem for quite a long while, and then flop down on to hands and knees again and crawl round to the other side of the table and pull himself up again — and then the toy is near to his hand. Success achieved!

While all this learning is going on it can be encouraged — or discouraged. There's a lot of bright intelligence waiting to be brought out and used. Again, if you praise the baby for the clever things he or she works out how to do, you are starting on the road to confident learning for the child. If, on the other hand, you are constantly on edge in case accidents or hurts may happen, the baby very soon learns to be hesitant and nervous, and learns more slowly. It is therefore very important to make sure that dangerous things are put away, such as poorly made toys and knitting needles and knives, and that electric plugs have safety covers, so that you are not for ever saying 'NO' and rushing to remove the baby from danger. Make the environment in your home as accident-proof as you can, by thinking ahead, and then enjoy your baby's adventurousness.

It is important also to consider stability in a young child's life. The stability of people is far more important than stability of place. Young children can take change of home, or change of circumstances as long as they have the same people supporting them. But if the people loving and supporting them change, then a familiar environment becomes more important than it ever was before.

For example, if you go out for the evening and take the baby with you, all will be well; if the baby wakes, there you are, familiar old mum and dad; the new surroundings are just some interesting new entertainment. If the baby is left at home with a known baby-sitter, all is well; if it wakes, the familiar person is still there. If the baby is left at home with an unknown baby-sitter, all is dicey; if it wakes, it faces the unfamiliar — and that's a crisis from the baby's point of view, but still the place is right. If the baby is left with a baby-sitter in an unfamiliar home, there is a double crisis of insecurity for the baby if it wakes — and you may have to be called back from your evening out.

Many fathers become much more interested in their children as they grow older. Unfortunately, some mothers resent the time that their partners spend playing with the baby, and may even envy the man's success with his child. They feel that they are left to do all the boring bits of cooking and cleaning while baby and father are just having fun. It is a pity when a mother feels this way, because the child's relationship of trust and friendship with his or her father is so very important. In fact, she has probably been wishing over the past months that her partner would take more time with the baby. Now that this is happening, it does mean the chance of a bit more free time for her, and she can take pride in the father-baby friendship which she has helped to make happen. It is because the baby is happy and interested that the father finds play so good, and that situation is very much her achievement because of the unfailing relationship the baby has with her.

The baby's first birthday is a milestone. Celebrating a whole year of caring since you gave birth should give you a feeling of quiet triumph. The result of all the patience you showed through the broken nights — the bewilderment of getting feeding going, the tiny spoonfuls of this and that new baby food to vary the diet, the non-stop nappy changing, the cuddles, the kisses, the smiles and the laughs — is sitting there, or gazing with sheer amazement at the one candle on the cake.

Looking back on the first year

Your baby's first birthday is a good time to look back and see where you have got to, and how you got there. Often the first thing that strikes you is how much your baby has grown since the momentous day of birth, and how much your own life has changed. Some of the mothers who attended a very lively antenatal class talked to me about their feelings as they looked back over the first year.

Mhari 'The first three months were a dream — and not altogether a good dream! After that it was good, and the last three months have been superb. Little Neil is mobile now, and can express himself and his emotions. He's such fun.

'He's always been a gorgeous baby, but for the first few months it was me who felt awful — I had piles and was desperately uncomfortable. I felt tired and draggy because of that. I enjoyed being a mum, but those first few weeks were *very* tiring. Neil's mobility made all the difference.

'My husband enjoys being a father, but he didn't enjoy waking at night one bit because he was working hard all day. He plays with the baby now a lot, and that's great. But I don't think he'd be so keen on his son if he had him all day and every day! When I was in bed with 'flu a week or two ago and he had to look after the house and the baby he was totally exhausted.

'I haven't felt shut in with the baby, and I didn't miss going out until Neil was about ten months old. My husband gets out more than I do, because he has evening meetings and plays sport. But now if we decide to go out together, or if I want to go out in the evening, my in-laws live very near us and they are delighted to baby-sit. I'm very lucky. We are expecting our second baby in about six months' time, and I wonder whether this next baby will be anything at all the same!'

Amanda 'The year has gone very quickly. I loved him straight away, and had no problems about that, but he didn't sleep well at first — and nor did I — so I was tired.

'I hadn't realized how strong my emotions would be when he was born — that absolute involvement with the baby. Right at the start, when he had to have physiotherapy and he cried, it really twisted me up. I couldn't get Andrew, my husband, to understand that if we went out, even though he could forget the baby for a few hours and trust that he was well looked after, I couldn't. Jamie was always on my mind. I couldn't even have a bath without wondering if he was all right while I was away from him.

'I didn't *want* to get away from him. I knew when I decided to breastfeed him that it would mean being tied down for months, but still I was totally unprepared for this emotional strength of involvement. I had problems with breastfeeding, lots of infections; I had mastitis almost every month at the beginning and I must have eaten masses of antibiotics. That was really wearing.

'My husband was not too sure about becoming a father before the baby was born. But he took to it straight away. He says being at the birth made all the difference; he felt involved with his son from then on. He handled Jamie well and is very gentle with him — he can almost be a bore about him to people now! But his involvement with Jamie is small compared to mine, because he's at work and he's involved with his work and works very hard.

'Communications with our son are much better now. I wouldn't have missed those early, more difficult days, but it's very nice now.'

Patsy 'I'm glad that first year's over! He's a gorgeous baby but he's only just started sleeping well. He's so different from my first baby, who was a sleeping baby. Mind you, this one was fine at first, and was settled into a happy routine until he was six months' old. But then he had to have operations — two hydroseals and a hernia — and they upset him very badly. He took months to settle again, and he started teething at about the same time which was very tough for him. Both he and I got very tired, and that was a hard time for us all, including my little boy.

'My husband's at sea, and hardly ever at home. While the baby was ill and upset he got desperately tired whenever he was at home, and said he was glad to go back to sea to get a sleep! I would have liked him home much more often because he's very domesticated and cooks wonderfully, and it's so much easier when there are two of you.

'Friends are wonderful. The class group has stayed in touch and I see them from time to time. But I have a lot of personal friends near me and they are terrific. I don't know what I would have done without friends.'

Linda 'This year has been easier than I ever imagined. I've had more time than I could have expected, this one being my second baby. I find it amazing that the two babies are so different — one sleeps and the other didn't; one is cuddly and the other wasn't. But they get on very well together, and now that the baby is a year old they are really playing together. They've always interested each other, and that's a big bonus.

'I did get very tired, because I myself had problems. I went for a cervical screen and they said I needed treating for some cell changes. I went home and thought "Oh no, why me?" The treatment was done, but it didn't heal well, so I had to have laser treatment. Now it's all cleared up and there's no sign of any more trouble. That's a wonderful relief. It made me very tired while it was all happening and the tiredness made me sharp with the older one when the baby cried, which wasn't fair to him. It's so easy to soothe the baby and be cross with the toddler and that's not right.

'My husband's not a baby person. He held the second baby much more than the first — I think he knows by now that a baby won't break! I got my slim figure back very quickly after the birth, and apart from the cervix business I felt fine, and the breast-feeding went easily.

'Some of my own activities had to be put on one side because of the baby, but that's to be expected. The group from the class has been good, since we kept meeting after our babies were born. Most of our friends through my husband's work are not at the same stage as we are, and have rather older children. When I am with them I don't want to talk babies all the time; they've mostly forgotten what their babies were like at my stage, and say that things went smoothly when I know fine that they didn't always! So it's very good to have another group of friends to talk babies to. It's been a good year.'

Fiona 'Really great! I've really enjoyed the year. I've been lucky, because Greg slept well right from the start, and by four months he was in a routine. It's all gone by the book.

'I've worked right up to the birth, and got back into shape almost at once, and kept in shape all the time I was breast-feeding. Funny, it was when I stopped breastfeeding that I started to put on a bit of weight!

'We've never really had a broken night. I didn't feel the first three months were hard, but they were in a way because he needed feeding every three hours, day and night. But I'm a very lazy person and I don't worry a lot, so I had Greg right beside me in his cot, and when he woke in the night I never once got out of bed, and my husband, Ewen, never woke up. I just put out my arms and took Greg into bed with me and breastfed him, then tucked him up again and we both went back to sleep. I never even bothered to change his nappy in the nights! In the morning Ewen got up and went to work, and I stayed in bed until Greg really woke up at about ten or eleven, so we both had lots of rest. If anyone came to the door on those mornings I always said I'd had a dreadful night with the baby, which explained why I was in my dressing gown so late!

'I had to stop breastfeeding when I went back to work — that was when Greg was 4½ months old. To start with it was only on Saturdays, when Ewen was at home. Then I went back three days a week, and on the two weekdays a super middle-aged lady who lives nearby looks after him, and he's really happy with her. On Saturdays with Ewen he has a muddlier day! Greg was very upset for about a week when I went back to work and stopped breastfeeding, and I felt dreadfully guilty, and wasn't at all comfortable myself because I weaned him too fast. But he went straight on to cow's milk, and the sort of bottle which has a teat shaped like a human nipple. He settled down very fast.

'There are one or two things I've done which I know other mothers maybe don't agree with. I use a dummy. It's not pretty to look at, but it works for him — or it did when he needed it at first. Also, when I put him down to sleep that was it — I didn't keep picking him up, so he soon learnt that that was sleep time. Of course if he wasn't well, or was in pain with teeth, that was different and I'd pick him up then and soothe him. I know that another baby might have a quite different temperament, but for Greg this system worked. Also I never got into the fuss of sterilizing things. I wash them well, of course, but he's got to get used to building his own antibodies to family germs, and I must say he's very healthy.

'The class I went to was a great help — we both enjoyed it, Ewen and I. Just the contact with other couples becoming parents for the first and second time was terrific. We've stayed friends, too, and see each other every month, and that's great.'

This group shows clearly how completely individual the experiences and reactions of new parents are, and how babies are individuals too. It's clear that any illness of baby or mother complicates the settling-in months and can easily overload the family unit when it is dealing with change and extra responsibility. But there's no one right way to become a family; each pair of parents will adapt to their baby in their own best way. What is beyond doubt is that each new family needs love and encouragement and support to achieve a comfortable balance, so that they can look back with happy achievement over their first year together.

NEW PERSPECTIVES ON PARENTING

Introduction

In a time of change it is tempting to look backwards with nostalgia to the familiar patterns of behaviour with which you grew up. If you had a happy and secure childhood yourself it's all too easy to moan about modern ways and pine for the old days; if you had an unhappy upbringing, you may be very glad of release from those old ways and yet you may feel rootless while carving out your own family style. Most new parents look back at their own childhood and want to retain the good things they benefited from, and discard the mistakes they think their parents made.

Sometimes, therefore, the mother and father may have strong views about the best way to bring up children, and their views and experiences can be diametrically opposite. When that is the case it is well worth talking about these differences before the baby is old enough to be bewildered or harmed by father and mother insisting on different family management.

The assumption is often made that all babies need the same treatment. This is not so, as you very soon learn. Of course there are basic needs that every baby is born with, for warmth and food and a secure person to care for him or her. And most intangible of all is the need for love. But babies' temperaments vary greatly; some are quick to settle into life at home, and some find the settling much more difficult.

A mother I know well, Alice, found her first baby very easy to soothe and feed. Within a month her daughter was sleeping through the night, and took to the family routine with ease. Her second baby was just the same, and Alice thought that her management of babies really worked well. Then her third child arrived, a much-wanted baby, born at home under ideal conditions and welcomed to the same handling as the older children. But this one was quite different, and came out into life fighting from the start, full of energy, and totally uninterested in sleep. Alice and John really didn't know what had hit them; all their theories about baby-care were swept away, nothing worked as it had for the older two, and Alice went around like a zombie for months until this lively sprite could crawl and get tired enough to drop off to sleep exhausted.

The most important thing is to keep an open mind from the start. There's a sense of great excitement about finding out what temperament your own baby has, and this excitement is usually tinged with fear and anxiety with your first baby. Most new parents have a short time when they feel all at sea, and may wonder how long this disorganized stage is going to last. It is then that you may fly to books in desperation, and there are so many detailed books of advice, as well as excellent women's magazines.

The way to use books and articles is the same as using advice — read everything, try the ideas that you think are good, and if they are helpful that's fine. If they don't work for your baby, discard them. Baby carriers, rocking cots, tapes of a mother's heart beat, tapes of soothing noises, lambskins, feeding hints, diet and herbs, sleeping habits and different styles of help — each and all may be the ideas which suit you and your baby. Parents and baby are a partnership. Babies bring up parents, not the other way round.

This is a wonderful time to be bringing up a family. There are not the same strict rules of behaviour that were in existence a century ago, and this means that each couple can choose and develop their own style of parenting.

However, freedom to choose your own way of parenting means

added responsibility. You have to decide on your own priorities. It is sometimes hard to be sure what is best for the family, especially for working mothers. The parents' needs and the baby's can appear to be opposing each other. For example, if you are breastfeeding your baby and very much enjoying doing so, and yet for financial reasons it would be helpful for you to go back to work part-time, you may be torn about how to decide for the best. Do you try to keep on breastfeeding and leave a bottle of expressed breastmilk for the baby-minder to give to your baby while you are at work? Do you wean the baby on to cow's milk and tackle the business of drying up your own supply? Do you abandon going back to work until the baby weans him or herself? Or do you take the baby with you to work, always supposing that conditions at your place of work allow this — and you want to do so?

The key factor is being able to look at your baby and make up your mind what is best for him or her. This first year is extraordinarily important for laying the basis of physical health and mental security for your child, and it is important not to lose sight of this in the upheaval of the early days after giving birth. Time and thought given to the baby now mean so much more freedom of choice later on. If your baby learns security and can rely on you when very new to the world, the base for brave adventuring into the wider world is firmly laid. Later, your toddler will be sure that even if you go away for a while, you will return.

Attitudes and society

Since this book was first written six years ago some disturbing things have happened in our society and have shaken our attitudes on child care. There have been many more cases reported of incredible and sickening violence towards babies and toddlers; there have been cases of neglect and children have been left for long hours alone at home, and there have been cases of sexual cruelty towards children by adults entrusted with their care.

Parents in the 1990s have to face a new fear — that someone with no reason but anger, frustration or wickedness may harm their child, out of the blue. Parents' anxiety levels have been, and are, wound up much higher by every such happening, and this anxiety may spread to our children.

But it is only when uncomfortable facts are publicly known that something can be done about them. As a society, we are beginning to respond to family needs. The setting up of such excellent work as Childline — the telephone network for distressed children — has made us aware of the horrifying amount of unhappiness in children. Various public bodies and support groups have been set up in order to give help to families under stress and in need of advice (— see *Useful addresses* section on page 191).

As individuals, an awareness of what has been happening to children in the headlines should force us to confront the crucial issue of child care. You should consider your role as a parent very carefully, taking into account what is going on in the world in which your child will grow up. Your own attitudes, moral values and personality will have direct effect on the baby.

You will discover that the change in pace and the adjustment to total responsibility for another's life, which is parenthood, can be a shock, and demanding. You will probably find that your own attitudes and values will change as your responsibility for your child grows.

How others may see us

New mothers are often accused of being boring. How can a woman who a few months ago was an avid reader of newspapers, a film buff, a keen theatre-goer, a bookworm, devoted to pop music, a cookery expert, a chess fiend, or keen on sport of any sort suddenly be so overwhelmingly interested in the smiles of a baby like any other baby, or the relative value of different disposable nappies, for heaven's sake? Old friends who shared the earlier interests are stunned by these new concerns, and often fail to realize that any new and absorbing interest is boring to those who haven't had the experience or felt the fascination.

Every new stage in life enlarges experience and pushes back horizons. New interests take over, new outlooks develop, and new friends inevitably follow. Language changes, and a person finds herself or himself on a wavelength with other people whom they had regarded as infinitely boring before.

It happens in education; nothing so boring and exclusive as the conversation of those who go on to university, for those who do not. It happens when you get a job and you suddenly find your own interests are different from those who have not got a job. It happens when you change your job or go into some new sphere, especially if the new job has its own jargon. How many of us have been bored to tears by hearing a friend go on and on about his job in computers? Or advertising, or medicine, or business sales, or journalism, or acting?

It happens with each new development in a person's life. Friendships are strained to breaking if one friend or the other falls in love and enters an exclusive world of his or her own. There is nothing so tedious as the conversation of someone deeply in love, or in a new relationship, or just married, or soldiering through a divorce. Overwhelming interest in what is happening to oneself tends to cut out the ability to listen to others — except others who share the experience or state of mind, and therefore understand.

Why is such new emancipation regarded by others in this negative way? Jealousy? Envy? A feeling of being shut out? Embarrassment at emotion honestly stated? Could it be that we simply despise family life? The rating for motherhood and fatherhood is certainly at an all-time low.

What about the children?

Women and men of even average sensitivity very soon learn to curb their enthusiasm for their babies and small children in adult company, until they have worked out whether the people they are with have an interest in parenthood. Some go further and speak disparagingly of their children so that they hide the pride and delight from those who might be turned off and bored. Many parents speak of their children as 'little monsters' and willingly imply that life with kids is hell, simply to avoid the perceived danger of being boring.

This is hard for their children. Since in childhood you can only learn your own self-worth through the way you are valued by your parents and your immediate circle of siblings and friends, it doesn't help your self-confidence to hear your parents go on and on about how your existence restricts and deprives them, and what a pest you are to bring up. The fact that your parents are really bursting with pride over producing you at all, and may be speaking that way because they are themselves afraid of being thought boring by their colleagues, doesn't dawn on you till much later, and after much heartache and self-doubt as you grow up.

We do not wear our children with pride. So of course society fails to value parenthood as a hugely important contribution that any ordinary individual can make to our country and the world. Yet it is the next generation whose future we hold in our hands.

As the child grows, he or she will probably be bored to death time and time again by its parents and the adults among whom it is growing up. Who has not seen a small child waiting and waiting in the street or a shop, while its parent talks interminably to another adult about interests which mean nothing to the child? Who has not seen such a child ask for attention and been told to shut up, or eventually get its hand away from the parent and move away, or do something more interesting from the child's viewpoint, and be slapped or told off as a result? How illogical parental behaviour must seem to a child's mind, and how impossible it must be to state your case to such powerful beings as your parents.

There is a danger we will become a society where children are at root regarded as possessions, not as people. But the opportunity to change such attitudes is open to us. It has always been open to parents to treat their children with respect and the quality of attention which they give naturally to other adults. We have all been children, so we should understand what children need and find interesting and worthwhile.

Men

Much depends on men. How highly does a man rate his job as a father to his children as against his job as a wage-earner? His success at his wage-earning job depends on the *quality* of his interest in it and the *attention* he gives to it — attention to detail and attention to the wider aspects of his work. His success as a parent depends on exactly the same. He may have little spontaneous interest in the details of baby-care, or babies themselves, but is he attentive to the wellbeing of the person or persons who are doing the caring for his child? A bank manager may have little interest in the boring balancing of money at the end of each day, but he is extremely careful about the quality of the staff who do that essential job, and therefore of the terms and conditions of their employment. If a man sees himself as the head of his household then he should have the same concern for the effectiveness of his establishment.

If he sees himself as an equal partner with the woman who shares his life and home, the same applies. They each have areas of preference, and parts of living which they do best; if both are best at earning money in satisfying work away from home then the needs of their children must be met by someone else and be carefully understood.

If, on the other hand, they both prefer to do the parenting work in the home, and find life more satisfying if they are helping children to grow and learn, then they must decide between them who does the essential job of earning money to keep the family going, It is work which must be done by someone, if you and your children are to eat and be clothed, let alone enjoy all the wider aspects of living such as education, travel and sport.

Our tradition is for the man to be the money-earner and the woman to be the home-maker, and to a very large extent that will probably continue, whatever changes are achieved by social, economic and political influence. At the start of parenthood, when your baby is born, there is no doubt that the mother is the very first person the baby needs and relies on for care and relationship, and life itself. The essential fatherliness needed at that stage is in support and encouragement for them both. The need for his fatherly involvement increases steadily as the baby grows and develops. It's not just a question of sharing the chores of washing and cooking and getting up to a baby at night; the more important need is for genuine interest in the child's wellbeing and concern for things to go well.

We pay little attention to bringing up and educating boys for fatherhood. Most new fathers have only had the role model of their own father to prepare them, and this can be frightening. A new baby is so small, and so instinctive; mothers *know* they are essential to their babies — men are not sure at first. Mothers are immediately involved with their baby — fathers may feel excluded. A father has the same weight of new responsibility as the mother, but over slightly different things at first. He realizes at once that he now has two dependents on him in a way that he has probably never experienced before, and he may doubt his resources, financially, practically and personally, because his parents have probably never talked to him about this weight of sudden care.

While he is giving support and encouragement to his baby's mother, the father is in need of support himself — from her, and from the friends and family round them. Not crushing sympathy, but encouragement and admiration for his fathering involvement with his child. Men have new freedom of choice, as well as women, and some men may cling to past ways and resist change until they see the benefits of new interests in their children. Fathers are so very important to children. Think of your own father. Whether he was there or not there, kind or unkind, remote or concerned, encouraging or deflating, he had a big influence on your growing up.

A new start

However much we try to think ahead and be wise in the way we handle our babies in the first year and on into childhood, we all make mistakes. We lose patience, get flustered and forget the longer perspectives in the daily hurly-burly. It's impossible to be perfect, and some of the mistakes we make will make us feel guilty, or ashamed, or be a source of bitter tears over a long time. Once I failed to see how lonely one of our five children was, even in a busy united family, because for a while she was the odd one out. It took a wise GP to alert me to what was happening to her, and it still makes me cringe to think of the unhappiness she went through which we could have avoided with more sensitivity. But you learn by mistakes, and we were alert to times when one or other child was the odd one out after that. Growing up is always painful at times, and growing up as a parent is no exception. But growth is life, and wise people never stop growing till they die.

Maybe if we thought in depth about the heavy weight of responsibility of parenting we might never take it on at all. So it is probably wise that it is in pregnancy that all these concerns and attitudes begin to be of overwhelming interest. Being a parent is the most important and influential job in the world, because the future is quite literally in your hands. Don't ever feel you are trapped by the past. A new baby is a new start, a whole new opportunity, an influence in the world of 30 years ahead. You may have started this baby for many different reasons, or for no reason at all, but be prepared for change.

The change can be quite dramatic. One mother I know was definite during her pregnancy that this baby would not change her way of life at all. 'I will not change my ways', she said, 'The baby must learn to fit into our lifestyle right from the beginning.' She didn't feel maternal at all and was very much her own woman, Yet when her baby was born she suddenly saw life totally differently, partly through the baby's eyes and partly through her instinctive response to the experience of giving birth. No mother I know has put more time and thought into the art of being a parent, with satisfying results.

For most of us the change is not so dramatically clear. We learn more slowly and by trial and error as much as by reason and planning. But learn we do, and the investment we put into being a parent in terms of time and thought and interest is richly rewarded by the growth and development of our babies, into children, and then teenagers and eventually adults. On the way we have fears and anxieties, and a great deal of warmth, companionship and inspiration, laughter and fun and friendship. Becoming a parent, starting a family, is full of promise.

Further reading

Pregnancy

Baby and Child by Penelope Leach (Penguin)

Meditations and Positive Thoughts for Pregnancy and Birth by Gilli Moorhawk (Piatkus)

Parents A-Z by Penelope Leach (Penguin)

Pregnancy and Childbirth by Sheila Kitzinger (Penguin)

Pregnancy Day by Day by Sheila Kitzinger with Vicky Bailey (Dorling Kindersley)

Childbirth

A Child is Born by Lennart Nilsson (Doubleday)

Being Born by Sheila Kitzinger (Dorling Kindersley)

Birth at Home by Sheila Kitzinger (Oxford University Press)

Birthrights: parents guide to modern childbirth by Sally Inch (Green Print)

Exercises for Childbirth by Johanna Roeber and Barbara Dale (Frances Lincoln)

Experience of Childbirth by Sheila Kitzinger (Penguin)

Freedom and Choice in Childbirth by Sheila Kitzinger (Penguin)

Giving Birth — how it really feels by Sheila Kitzinger (Gollancz)

Home Birth by Sheila Kitzinger (Dorling Kindersley)

Midwife Challenge by Sheila Kitzinger (Pandora Press)

Sensitive Midwifery by Caroline Flint (Butterworth Heinemann)

First Year

Babyhood: infant development from birth by Penelope Leach (Penguin)

Experience of Breastfeeding by Sheila Kitzinger (Penguin)

Year After Childbirth by Sheila Kitzinger (Oxford University Press)

General

A Woman in Your own Right by Anne Dickson (Quartet)

Bereavement: studies of grief in adult life by Colin Murray Parkes (Routledge)

Children First by Penelope Leach (Michael Joseph)

Coping with a Miscarriage by Hank Pizer and Christine O'Brien Palinski (Jill Norman)

How a First Child Changes a Marriage by Dr Jay Belsky and John Kelly (Vermilion Press)

Nature's Child by Leslie Kenton (Ebury)

Ourselves as Mothers by Sheila Kitzinger (Bantam Books)

Positive Parenting by Pat Rees (Attic Press)

Stress and Relaxation by Jane Madders (Optima, Little Brown)

The Complete Baby and Toddler Meal Planner by Annabel Karmel (Ebury)

The Crying Baby by Sheila Kitzinger (Penguin)

The Food Combining Diet by Kathryn Marsden (Thorsons)

The Great Ormond Street Book of Baby and Childcare (Bodley Head)

The Massage Book by George Downing (Penguin)

The Road Less Travelled by M Scott Peck (Century)

Toddler Taming by Dr Christopher Green (Vermilion Press)

Understanding Your Baby by Lisa Miller of the Tavistock Clinic (Rosendale Press)

Useful addresses

Breastfeeding

National Childbirth Trust
Alexandra House
Oldham Terrace
Acton
London W3 6NH
081-992 8637

La Lèche League
BM 3424
London WC1N 3XX
071-242 1278

Child Abuse

NSPCC
Headquarters
42 Curtain Road
London EC2A 3NH
071-825 2500
Helpline: 0800 800500
(available 24 hours)

Parents Against Injustice (PAIN)
3 Riverside Business Park
Stansted
Essex CM24 8PL
0279 647171

(National charity providing specialist advice and support solely to those who state they have been mistakenly involved in investigations of alleged child abuse)

Child care

Family Rights Group
(England & Wales)
The Print House
18 Ashwin Street
London E8 3DL
Helpline: 071-249 0008
(1.30pm-3.30pm Mon-Fri)

(Promotes partnerships between families and child care agencies)

Pre-School Playgroups Association
61-63 Kings Cross Road
London WC1X 9LL
071-833 0991
Helpline: 071-837 5513
10am-5pm Mon-Fri
(answerphone 24 hours)

(For all parents seeking child care facilities)

Crying baby

CRY-SIS
BM CRY-SIS
London WC1N 3XX
071-404 5011 24 hours

(Offers self-help and support for families with excessively crying, sleepless and demanding babies and toddlers)

Death of a baby

CRUSE (Bereavement Care)
Cruse House
126 Sheen Road
Richmond
Surrey
TW9 1UR
081-940 4818
Helpline: 081-332 7227
9.30am-5pm Mon-Fri

Foundation for the Study of Infant Deaths
Head Office
35 Belgrave Square
London SW1X 8QB
071-235 0965
Cot Death Helpline:
071-235 1721
(Mon-Sun 24 hours)

SANDS (Stillbirth and Neonatal Death Society)
28 Portland Place
London W1N 4DE
071-436 5881

The Compassionate Friends
53 North Street
Bristol BS3 1EN
0272 665202
Helpline: 0272 539639
(9.30am-5pm Mon-Fri)

Education and preparation for pregnancy and birth

National Childbirth Trust
Alexandra House
Oldham Terrace
Acton
London W3 6NH
081-992 8637

Active Birth Centre
55 Dartmouth Park Road
London NW5 1SL
071-267 3006

Brook Advisory Centres
153A East Street
London SE17 2SD
071-708 1234
Helpline: 071 617 8000
(available 24 hours)

LIFE
LIFE House
1A Newbold Terrace
Leamington Spa
Warwicks CV32 4EA
Helpline: 0926 311511
(9am-9pm Mon-Sun)

Lifeline Pregnancy Care
Cae Bach
4 Pant y Wennol
Bodafon
Llandudno
Gwynedd LL30 3DS
0492 543741

Wellbeing
27 Sussex Place
Regents Park
London NW1 4SP
071-262 5337
Eating in Pregnancy Helpline:
0742 424084 24 hours

Handicap

Association for Spina Bifida and Hydrocephalus
ASBH House
42 Park Road
Peterborough PE1 2UQ
0733 555988

Contact-a-Family
170 Tottenham Court Road
London W1P 0HA
Helpline: 071-383 3555
(9am-5.30pm and answerphone)

(Links families with disabled children into neighbourhood self-help groups)

DIAL UK (Disablement Information and Advice Line)
Park Lodge
St Catherine's Hospital
Tickhill Road
Balby
Doncaster
South Yorkshire DN4 8QN
0302 310123 9am-5pm
Mon-Thurs, 9am-4pm Fri
and answerphone

(Free, independent advice on all aspects of disability)

Homebased Parents

Full Time Mothers
PO Box 186
London SW3 5RF
071-485 4531 10am-5pm
Mon-Fri and answerphone

Midwives

Association of Radical Midwives
62 Greetby Hill
Ormskirk
Lancashire L39 2DT
0695 572776

Independent Midwives Association
Nightingale Cottage
Shamblehurst Lane
Botley
Hampshire SO3 2BY
0703 694429

(Please send A5 SAE for details of independent midwives)

Miscarriage

Miscarriage Association (Acknowledging Pregnancy Loss)
Head Office
c/o Clayton Hospital
Northgate
Wakefield
West Yorkshire WF1 3JS
0924 200799
answerphone after hours

One-parent families

Gingerbread
35 Wellington Street
London WC2E 7BN
Adviceline: 071 240 0953
(11am-2pm Mon-Fri)

Holiday Care Service
2 Old Bank Chambers
Station Road
Horley
Surrey RH6 9HW
Helpline: 0293 774535
9am-6pm Mon-Fri
(answerphone out of hours)

(Information about holidays for one-parent families)

National Council for one-parent families
255 Kentish Town Road
London NW5 2LX
071-267 1361

Postnatal problems

Association for Post Natal Illness
25 Jerdan Place
Fulham
London SW6 1BE
Helpline: 071-386 0868
(10am-5pm Mon-Fri)

(Telephone support on a one-to-one basis for women suffering with Post Natal Depression, from women who have recovered from it. Send SAE for free information pack.)

Home-Start Consultancy
2 Salisbury Road
Leicester LE1 7QR
0533 554988

MAMA (Meet-a-Mum Association)
14 Willis Road
Croydon
Surrey CRO 2XX
081-665 0357

Helpline (for mums with Post Natal Depression):
081-656 7318 3.30pm-11pm Mon-Fri; 11am-8pm Sat-Sun

Premature babies

NIPPERS (National Information for Parents of Prematures)
17-21 Emerald Street
London WC1N 3QL
071-831 9393

Relationship problems

Family Planning Association
27-35 Mortimer Street
London W1N 7RJ
071-636 7866

(help with sexual problems)

Institute of Marital Studies
Tavistock Centre
120 Belsize Lane
London NW3 5BA
071-435 7111

London Marriage Guidance Council
76a New Cavendish Street
London W1M 7LB
071-580 1087

Relate - National Marriage Guidance
Herbert Gray College
Little Church Street
Rugby
Warwickshire CV21 3AP
0788 573241

William Kyle Centre
Westminster Pastoral Foundation
23 Kensington Square
London W8 5HN
071-376 2404

Stress

Exploring Parenthood (EP)
Latimer Education Centre
194 Freston Road
London W10 6TT
081-960 1678

(Professional support and advice)

Home Start UK
2 Salisbury Road
Leicester LE7 7QR
0533 554988
(10am-5pm Mon-Fri)

(Volunteers offer regular support, friendship and practical help to young families under stress)

Parentline
Westbury House
57 Hart Road
Thundersley
Essex SS7 3PP
Helpline: 0268 757077 9am-6pm Mon-Fri; 10am-2pm Sat (afterhours numbers supplied on answerphone)

Parent Network
44-46 Caversham Road
London NW5 2DS
071-485 8535

Suppliers of Lambskins

Winganna Natural Products
St Ishmaels
Haverfordwest
Dyfed
SA62 3DL
0646 636403

Twins

TAMBA (Twins and Multiple Births Association)
PO Box 30
Little Sutton
South Wirral L66 1TH
051 348 0020
Helpline: 0732 868000
6pm-11pm Mon-Fri;
10am-11pm Sat-Sun

Welfare

Family Service Unit
207 Old Marylebone Road
London NW1 5QP
071-402 5175

(Promotes the welfare of severely disadvantaged families through social work intervention and influencing national social policy)

Family Welfare Association
501-505 Kingsland Road
London E8 4AU
071-254 6251

(Provides practical, emotional and financial support to families in need)

Work outside the home

Parents at Work
77 Holloway Road
London N7 8JZ
Helpline: 071-700 5771
(9am-1pm, 2pm-4pm Tues, Thurs and Fri)

Index